MADLIBS®

MAD LIBS MANIA

MAD LIBS®

MAD LIBS MANIA

concept created by Roger Price & Leonard Stern

PSS!
PRICE STERN SLOAN
An Imprint of Penguin Group (USA) LLC

PRICE STERN SLOAN
Published by the Penguin Group
Penguin Group (USA) LLC, 375 Hudson Street, New York, New York 10014, USA

USA | Canada | UK | Ireland | Australia | New Zealand | India | South Africa | China

penguin.com
A Penguin Random House Company

Mad Libs format and text copyright © 1996, 2001, 2008, 2009, 2012, 2014, 2015 by Price Stern Sloan,
an imprint of Penguin Group (USA) LLC. All rights reserved.

Mad Libs Mania published in 2015 by Price Stern Sloan, a division of Penguin Young Readers Group,
345 Hudson Street, New York, New York 10014.
Printed in the USA.

Mad Libs Mania ISBN 978-0-8431-8289-7

11 13 15 17 19 20 18 16 14 12

MAD LIBS®

GRAB BAG
MAD LIBS

by Roger Price & Leonard Stern

PSS!

PRICE STERN SLOAN

An Imprint of Penguin Group (USA) LLC

INSTRUCTIONS

MAD LIBS® is a game for people who don't like games!
It can be played by one, two, three, four, or forty.

● RIDICULOUSLY SIMPLE DIRECTIONS

In this tablet you will find stories containing blank spaces where words are left out. One player, the READER, selects one of these stories. The READER does not tell anyone what the story is about. Instead, he/she asks the other players, the WRITERS, to give him/her words. These words are used to fill in the blank spaces in the story.

● TO PLAY

The READER asks each WRITER in turn to call out a word—an adjective or a noun or whatever the space calls for—and uses them to fill in the blank spaces in the story. The result is a MAD LIBS® game.

When the READER then reads the completed MAD LIBS® game to the other players, they will discover that they have written a story that is fantastic, screamingly funny, shocking, silly, crazy, or just plain dumb—depending upon which words each WRITER called out.

● EXAMPLE (Before and After)

" _____ !" he said _____
  EXCLAMATION   ADVERB

as he jumped into his convertible _____ and
                                     NOUN

drove off with his _____ wife.
                   ADJECTIVE

" *Ouch* !" he said *stupidly*
  EXCLAMATION   ADVERB

as he jumped into his convertible *cat* and
                                     NOUN

drove off with his *brave* wife.
                   ADJECTIVE

MAD LIBS®

QUICK REVIEW

In case you have forgotten what adjectives, adverbs, nouns, and verbs are, here is a quick review:

An ADJECTIVE describes something or somebody. *Lumpy, soft, ugly, messy,* and *short* are adjectives.

An ADVERB tells how something is done. It modifies a verb and usually ends in "ly." *Modestly, stupidly, greedily,* and *carefully* are adverbs.

A NOUN is the name of a person, place, or thing. *Sidewalk, umbrella, bridle, bathtub,* and *nose* are nouns.

A VERB is an action word. *Run, pitch, jump,* and *swim* are verbs. Put the verbs in past tense if the directions say PAST TENSE. *Ran, pitched, jumped,* and *swam* are verbs in the past tense.

When we ask for A PLACE, we mean any sort of place: a country or city *(Spain, Cleveland)* or a room *(bathroom, kitchen).*

An EXCLAMATION or SILLY WORD is any sort of funny sound, gasp, grunt, or outcry, like *Wow!, Ouch!, Whomp!, Ick!,* and *Gadzooks!*

When we ask for specific words, like a NUMBER, a COLOR, an ANIMAL, or a PART OF THE BODY, we mean a word that is one of those things, like *seven, blue, horse,* or *head.*

When we ask for a PLURAL, it means more than one. For example, *cat* pluralized is *cats.*

INTERVIEW WITH A ROCK STAR

PLURAL NOUN _____

PLURAL NOUN _____

NOUN _____

COLOR _____

VERB _____

ADJECTIVE _____

NOUN _____

NOUN _____

ADJECTIVE _____

ADJECTIVE _____

NUMBER _____

ADJECTIVE _____

ADJECTIVE _____

ADJECTIVE _____

NOUN _____

VERB _____

Now you've created your own hilarious MAD LIBS® game!

MAD LIBS®
INTERVIEW WITH A ROCK STAR

QUESTION: Whatever made you choose the name "The Psycho

_____" for your group?
　　PLURAL NOUN

ANSWER: All the other good names like the "Rolling _____,"
　　　　　　　　　　　　　　　　　　　　　　　　　　　PLURAL NOUN

"_____ Jam," and "_____ Floyd" were taken.
　　NOUN　　　　　　　　　　　　　COLOR

QUESTION: You not only _____ songs, but you play many
　　　　　　　　　　　　　　　VERB

_____ instruments, don't you?
　ADJECTIVE

ANSWER: Yes. I play the electric _____, the bass _____,
　　　　　　　　　　　　　　　　　NOUN　　　　　　　　　　　NOUN

and the _____ keyboard.
　　　　　ADJECTIVE

QUESTION: You now have a/an _____ song that is number
　　　　　　　　　　　　　　ADJECTIVE

_____ on the _____ charts. What was the inspiration for
　NUMBER　　　　　　ADJECTIVE

this _____ song?
　　ADJECTIVE

ANSWER: Believe it or not, it was a/an _____ song that my
　　　　　　　　　　　　　　　　　　　ADJECTIVE

mother used to sing to me when it was time for _____, and it
　　　　　　　　　　　　　　　　　　　　　　　NOUN

never failed to _____ me to sleep.
　　　　　　VERB

HAVE I GOT
A GIRAFFE FOR YOU!

_____ PLURAL NOUN

_____ PLURAL NOUN

_____ PART OF THE BODY

_____ NUMBER

_____ PLURAL NOUN

_____ PART OF THE BODY

_____ TYPE OF LIQUID

_____ PART OF THE BODY (PLURAL)

_____ PART OF THE BODY

_____ ADJECTIVE

_____ PLURAL NOUN

_____ ADJECTIVE

_____ ADJECTIVE

_____ VERB ENDING IN "ING"

_____ NOUN

_____ PLURAL NOUN

_____ NOUN

Giraffes have aroused the curiosity of _____ since earliest times.

PLURAL NOUN

The giraffe is the tallest of all living _____, but scientists are

PLURAL NOUN

unable to explain how it got its long _____. The giraffe's

PART OF THE BODY

tremendous height, which might reach _____ _____,

NUMBER   PLURAL NOUN

comes mostly from its legs and _____. If a giraffe wants to

PART OF THE BODY

take a drink of _____ from the ground, it has to spread its

TYPE OF LIQUID

_____ far apart in order to reach down and lap up the

PART OF THE BODY (PLURAL)

water with its huge _____. The giraffe has _____

PART OF THE BODY   ADJECTIVE

ears that are sensitive to the faintest _____, and it has a/an

PLURAL NOUN

_____ sense of smell and sight. When attacked, a giraffe can put

ADJECTIVE

up a/an _____ fight by _____ out with its hind

ADJECTIVE   VERB ENDING IN "ING"

legs and using its head like a sledge _____. Finally, a giraffe can

NOUN

gallop at more than thirty _____ an hour when pursued and can

PLURAL NOUN

outrun the fastest _____.

NOUN

THE OLYMPICS

_____ NOUN

_____ PLURAL NOUN

_____ ADJECTIVE

_____ PLURAL NOUN

_____ PLURAL NOUN

_____ NUMBER

_____ ADJECTIVE

_____ ADJECTIVE

_____ NOUN

_____ ADJECTIVE

_____ VERB ENDING IN "S"

_____ PART OF THE BODY

_____ NOUN

_____ ADJECTIVE

_____ PLURAL NOUN

_____ PLURAL NOUN

MAD LIBS

THE OLYMPICS

Every two years, countries from all over the _____ send their best
                                              NOUN

_____ to compete in _____ games and win _____.
PLURAL NOUN   ADJECTIVE   PLURAL NOUN

These events are called the Olympic _____, and they started
                                     PLURAL NOUN

_____ years ago in _____ Greece. When a winner
NUMBER   ADJECTIVE

receives his or her _____ medal at the games, the national
                    ADJECTIVE

_____ of his or her country is played by a/an _____
NOUN   ADJECTIVE

band. As the band _____, the citizens of that country put
                  VERB ENDING IN "S"

their _____ to their chest and join in the singing of their
      PART OF THE BODY

national _____. Thanks to television, these _____ events
         NOUN   ADJECTIVE

can now be watched by over a billion _____ throughout the world
                                      PLURAL NOUN

every two _____.
          PLURAL NOUN

From GRAB BAG MAD LIBS® • Copyright © 1996, 2001 by Price Stern Sloan,
an imprint of Penguin Group (USA) LLC, 345 Hudson Street, New York, NY 10014.

HOME SWEET HOME

NOUN _____

PART OF THE BODY _____

NUMBER _____

NOUN _____

COLOR _____

ADJECTIVE _____

NOUN _____

NOUN _____

PLURAL NOUN _____

NOUN _____

NOUN _____

ADJECTIVE _____

NOUN _____

ADVERB _____

PART OF THE BODY _____

VERB ENDING IN "ING" _____

ADJECTIVE _____

MAD LIBS®

HOME SWEET HOME

Some people are fond of the saying, "Home is where you hang your

_____ ." Others say, "Home is where the _____
   NOUN   PART OF THE BODY

is." As for me, even though my home is a rustic, _____-story
                                                      NUMBER

_____ home with a/an _____ picket fence surrounding
   NOUN   COLOR

it, I think of it as my _____ castle. Perched on a/an
                              ADJECTIVE

_____ overlooking a babbling _____ and surrounded by
   NOUN   NOUN

a forest of huge _____, my home offers me _____ and
                   PLURAL NOUN   NOUN

tranquility. Each and every _____ I look forward to coming back
                              NOUN

to my _____ home, where my faithful _____ will
         ADJECTIVE   NOUN

_____ greet me by wagging its _____ and
   ADVERB   PART OF THE BODY

_____ all over me. I just love my home _____ home.
VERB ENDING IN "ING"   ADJECTIVE

MAD LIBS® is fun to play with friends, but you can also play it by yourself! To begin with, DO NOT look at the story on the page below. Fill in the blanks on this page with the words called for. Then, using the words you have selected, fill in the blank spaces in the story.

Now you've created your own hilarious MAD LIBS® game!

INTERVIEW WITH A COMEDIAN

NOUN _____

ADJECTIVE _____

ADJECTIVE _____

NOUN _____

NUMBER _____

PLURAL NOUN _____

NOUN _____

VERB _____

VERB _____

PLURAL NOUN _____

PLURAL NOUN _____

ADJECTIVE _____

NOUN _____

MAD LIBS®
INTERVIEW WITH A COMEDIAN

QUESTION: Were you always a stand-up _____ ?
NOUN

ANSWER: No. I had many _____ jobs in my _____
ADJECTIVE   ADJECTIVE

lifetime. I started out as a used _____ salesperson, and then for
NOUN

_____ years, I sold ladies' _____ .
NUMBER   PLURAL NOUN

QUESTION: When did you discover you were a funny _____
NOUN

who could make people _____ out loud?
VERB

ANSWER: It was in school. The first time our teacher had us do show and

_____ , I made the _____ in my class laugh so hard
VERB   PLURAL NOUN

they fell out of their _____ .
PLURAL NOUN

QUESTION: How would you describe your _____ act?
ADJECTIVE

ANSWER: I am a thinking person's _____ .
NOUN

MAD LIBS® is fun to play with friends, but you can also play it by yourself! To begin with, DO NOT look at the story on the page below. Fill in the blanks on this page with the words called for. Then, using the words you have selected, fill in the blank spaces in the story.

Now you've created your own hilarious MAD LIBS® game!

MOVIES SHOULD BE FUN

PLURAL NOUN _____

ADJECTIVE _____

PLURAL NOUN _____

NOUN _____

ADJECTIVE _____

NOUN _____

NOUN _____

PERSON IN ROOM (MALE) _____

A PLACE _____

ADJECTIVE _____

PERSON IN ROOM _____

PERSON IN ROOM _____

ADJECTIVE _____

PLURAL NOUN _____

PART OF THE BODY (PLURAL) _____

MAD LIBS®

MOVIES SHOULD BE FUN

In recent years, there have been too many disaster movies in which tall

_____ catch on fire, _____ dinosaurs come to life, and
  PLURAL NOUN   ADJECTIVE

huge _____ attack people in the ocean, making you afraid to get
      PLURAL NOUN

out of your _____ in the morning. Movie fans ask why we can't
         NOUN

have more _____ pictures like *It's a Wonderful* _____,
      ADJECTIVE   NOUN

Gone with the _____, or *Mr.* _____ *Goes to (the)*
           NOUN   PERSON IN ROOM (MALE)

_____. These films made you feel _____ all over.
   A PLACE   ADJECTIVE

These same fans also ask why we can't have more funny films with comedians

such as Laurel and _____, and Abbott and _____.
        PERSON IN ROOM   PERSON IN ROOM

These _____ performers gave us great slapstick _____
     ADJECTIVE   PLURAL NOUN

that still makes our _____ ache from laughing.
       PART OF THE BODY (PLURAL)

MAD LIBS® is fun to play with friends, but you can also play it by yourself! To begin with, DO NOT look at the story on the page below. Fill in the blanks on this page with the words called for. Then, using the words you have selected, fill in the blank spaces in the story.

Now you've created your own hilarious MAD LIBS® game!

COOL IT

PLURAL NOUN _____

ADJECTIVE _____

NOUN _____

ADJECTIVE _____

NOUN _____

NOUN _____

NOUN _____

ADJECTIVE _____

VERB ENDING IN "ING" _____

NOUN _____

ADJECTIVE _____

NOUN _____

VERB _____

MAD LIBS®

COOL IT

Weather plays an important part in our daily _____. What is
PLURAL NOUN

weather, anyway? According to _____ scientists, who are known
ADJECTIVE

as meteorologists, weather is what the air is like at any time of the

_____. It doesn't matter if the air is cold, hot, or _____,
NOUN   ADJECTIVE

it's all weather. Weather changes from hour to _____, from day to
NOUN

_____, from season to _____, and from year to
NOUN   NOUN

_____. Daily changes in weather are caused by _____
NOUN   ADJECTIVE

storms _____ across the earth. Seasonal changes are from the
VERB ENDING IN "ING"

earth moving around the _____. When the vapors in _____
NOUN   ADJECTIVE

clouds condense, we have _____ and snow. Whether you like it or
NOUN

not, weather is here to _____.
VERB

GOING TO TOWN

LAST NAME
_____

ADJECTIVE
_____

PLURAL NOUN
_____

ADJECTIVE
_____

PERSON IN ROOM
_____

PLURAL NOUN
_____

PLURAL NOUN
_____

ADJECTIVE
_____

NOUN
_____

NUMBER
_____

VERB ENDING IN "ING"
_____

ADJECTIVE
_____

ADJECTIVE
_____

ADJECTIVE
_____

NOUN
_____

NOUN
_____

MAD LIBS®

GOING TO TOWN

THE ART SCENE

Today the _____ Gallery presents a series of _____
           LAST NAME   ADJECTIVE

landscape paintings and still-life _____ by the _____
                                    PLURAL NOUN   ADJECTIVE

artist, _____. These beautiful _____ will be on
         PERSON IN ROOM   PLURAL NOUN

exhibition for the next three _____.
                               PLURAL NOUN

MUSIC

Tonight marks the _____ debut of the all-_____ choir
                   ADJECTIVE   NOUN

of _____ great _____ voices. This _____
    NUMBER   VERB ENDING IN "ING"   ADJECTIVE

ensemble will present _____ renditions of such _____
                       ADJECTIVE   ADJECTIVE

children's songs as "Twinkle Twinkle Little _____" and "Old
                                             NOUN

MacDonald Had a/an _____."
                    NOUN

THE THREE MUSKETEERS

_____ ADJECTIVE

_____ PLURAL NOUN

_____ ADJECTIVE

_____ NOUN

_____ ADJECTIVE

_____ NOUN

_____ NOUN

_____ PLURAL NOUN

_____ NOUN

_____ PERSON IN ROOM

_____ PLURAL NOUN

_____ ADJECTIVE

_____ NOUN

_____ NOUN

_____ PLURAL NOUN

_____ NOUN

MAD LIBS®

THE THREE MUSKETEERS

There is no more rousing story in _____ literature than *The*
ADJECTIVE

Three _____. This _____ romance by the great French
PLURAL NOUN _ADJECTIVE_

_____ Alexander Dumas, tells the story of D' Artagnan, a/an
NOUN

_____ young _____ who arrives in 17th-century Paris
ADJECTIVE _NOUN_

riding a/an _____ with only three _____ in his pocket.
NOUN _PLURAL NOUN_

Determined to be in the service of the _____ who rules all of
NOUN

France, he duels with Athos, Pathos, and _____, three of the
PERSON IN ROOM

king's best _____. Eventually, these swordsmen and D' Artagnan
PLURAL NOUN

save their _____ king from being overthrown and losing his
ADJECTIVE

_____. Over the years, *The Three Musketeers* has been made into a
NOUN

stage _____, two motion _____, and, most recently,
NOUN _PLURAL NOUN_

into a Broadway _____.
NOUN

MAD LIBS® is fun to play with friends, but you can also play it by yourself! To begin with, DO NOT look at the story on the page below. Fill in the blanks on this page with the words called for. Then, using the words you have selected, fill in the blank spaces in the story.

Now you've created your own hilarious MAD LIBS® game!

SNOW WHITE

_____ PLURAL NOUN

_____ PLURAL NOUN

_____ ADJECTIVE

_____ PLURAL NOUN

_____ ADJECTIVE

_____ NOUN

_____ NOUN

_____ ADJECTIVE

_____ ADJECTIVE

_____ PLURAL NOUN

_____ NOUN

_____ COLOR

_____ NOUN

_____ PART OF THE BODY

_____ ADVERB

MAD LIBS®

SNOW WHITE

One of the most popular fairy _____ of all time is *Snow White*
                                    PLURAL NOUN

and the Seven _____. Snow White is a princess whose _____
                 PLURAL NOUN   ADJECTIVE

beauty threatens her stepmother, the queen, and her two step-_____,
                                                              PLURAL NOUN

who are very _____. Snow White is forced to flee from the
                ADJECTIVE

_____ in which she lives and hide in the nearby _____.
   NOUN   NOUN

Once there, she is discovered by _____ animals who guide her to
                                      ADJECTIVE

the _____ cottage of the seven dwarfs. The dwarfs come home
       ADJECTIVE

from digging in their mine and discover Snow White asleep in their

_____. The dwarfs take care of her until a prince, who has traveled
 PLURAL NOUN

the four corners of the _____ in search of Snow _____,
                            NOUN   COLOR

arrives and gives her a magical _____ on her _____,
                                    NOUN   PART OF THE BODY

which miraculously brings her back to life. Snow White and the prince live

_____ ever after.
    ADVERB

MAD LIBS® is fun to play with friends, but you can also play it by yourself! To begin with, DO NOT look at the story on the page below. Fill in the blanks on this page with the words called for. Then, using the words you have selected, fill in the blank spaces in the story.

Now you've created your own hilarious MAD LIBS® game!

MAGIC, ANYONE?

_____ PLURAL NOUN

_____ ADJECTIVE

_____ ADJECTIVE

_____ NOUN

_____ NOUN

_____ NOUN

_____ NOUN

_____ ADJECTIVE

_____ PART OF THE BODY

_____ PLURAL NOUN

_____ ADJECTIVE

_____ NOUN

_____ ADJECTIVE

_____ NOUN

_____ PART OF THE BODY (PLURAL)

_____ PART OF THE BODY

_____ PLURAL NOUN

MAD LIBS®

MAGIC, ANYONE?

_____ of all ages enjoy watching _____ magicians
   PLURAL NOUN   ADJECTIVE

perform their _____ tricks. Every man, woman, and _____
           ADJECTIVE   NOUN

loves to see a magician pull a/an _____ out of a hat, saw a live
                              NOUN

_____ in half, or make a huge _____ disappear into
  NOUN   NOUN

_____ air. Audiences love when magicians perform sleight of
  ADJECTIVE

_____ with a deck of _____, a/an _____
PART OF THE BODY   PLURAL NOUN   ADJECTIVE

coin, or a silk _____. The greatest of all magicians was the
            NOUN

_____ Harry Houdini, who was able to escape from a locked
  ADJECTIVE

_____ even though his _____ were tied
  NOUN   PART OF THE BODY (PLURAL)

behind his _____ and his feet were wrapped in iron _____.
     PART OF THE BODY   PLURAL NOUN

MAD LIBS® is fun to play with friends, but you can also play it by yourself! To begin with, DO NOT look at the story on the page below. Fill in the blanks on this page with the words called for. Then, using the words you have selected, fill in the blank spaces in the story.

Now you've created your own hilarious MAD LIBS® game!

THE BIG GAME

PLURAL NOUN _____

PERSON IN ROOM _____

NOUN _____

LAST NAME _____

PLURAL NOUN _____

A PLACE _____

PLURAL NOUN _____

A PLACE _____

PLURAL NOUN _____

NOUN _____

ADJECTIVE _____

ADJECTIVE _____

NOUN _____

NOUN _____

NOUN _____

VERB _____

ADJECTIVE _____

MAD LIBS®

THE BIG GAME

To be read with great enthusiasm!

Hello there, sports _____ ! This is _____ , talking to
                       PLURAL NOUN   PERSON IN ROOM

you from the press _____ in _____ Stadium, where
                        NOUN   LAST NAME

57,000 cheering _____ have gathered to watch (the) _____ .
                   PLURAL NOUN   A PLACE

_____ take on (the) _____ _____ . Even
  PLURAL NOUN   A PLACE   PLURAL NOUN

though the _____ is shining, it's a/an _____ cold day
               NOUN   ADJECTIVE

with the temperature in the _____ 20s. A strong _____
                                ADJECTIVE   NOUN

is blowing fiercely across the playing _____ that will definitely
                                            NOUN

affect the passing _____ . We'll be back for the opening
                        NOUN

_____ -off after a few words from our _____ sponsor.
    VERB   ADJECTIVE

MAD LIBS® is fun to play with friends, but you can also play it by yourself! To begin with, DO NOT look at the story on the page below. Fill in the blanks on this page with the words called for. Then, using the words you have selected, fill in the blank spaces in the story.

Now you've created your own hilarious MAD LIBS® game!

THINGS TO DO
THIS WEEKEND

LAST NAME _____

ADJECTIVE _____

PLURAL NOUN _____

PLURAL NOUN _____

NOUN _____

ADJECTIVE _____

NOUN _____

ADVERB _____

NOUN _____

ADJECTIVE _____

PLURAL NOUN _____

PERSON IN ROOM _____

ADJECTIVE _____

NOUN _____

ADJECTIVE _____

ADJECTIVE _____

NOUN _____

NOUN _____

ADJECTIVE _____

MAD LIBS®
THINGS TO DO THIS WEEKEND

FILM

_____ Theaters offers a/an _____ program of foreign
  LAST NAME   ADJECTIVE

_____ never before seen in American _____. The first
  PLURAL NOUN   PLURAL NOUN

film to be shown will be *Henry and the* _____. This is the
                                        NOUN

_____ love story of a man and his _____. It will be
  ADJECTIVE   NOUN

shown _____ until the end of the _____.
         ADVERB   NOUN

STAGE

Appearing in our _____ theater for the next three _____
             ADJECTIVE   PLURAL NOUN

is _____, that very _____ star of stage, screen, and
   PERSON IN ROOM   ADJECTIVE

_____. He/she will be appearing with our _____
  NOUN   ADJECTIVE

repertory company in nightly performances of William Shakespeare's

_____ comedy, *A Midsummer Night's* _____. Tickets
  ADJECTIVE   NOUN

can be purchased now at the _____ office by telephone, fax, or
                       NOUN

_____ card.
  ADJECTIVE

MAD LIBS® is fun to play with friends, but you can also play it by yourself! To begin with, DO NOT look at the story on the page below. Fill in the blanks on this page with the words called for. Then, using the words you have selected, fill in the blank spaces in the story.

Now you've created your own hilarious MAD LIBS® game!

SCENE FROM A
HORROR PICTURE

ADJECTIVE _____

PART OF THE BODY _____

PLURAL NOUN _____

NOUN _____

ADJECTIVE _____

PLURAL NOUN _____

EXCLAMATION _____

NOUN _____

PART OF THE BODY _____

PERSON IN ROOM _____

NOUN _____

PART OF THE BODY _____

ADJECTIVE _____

VERB _____

ADVERB _____

NOUN _____

NOUN _____

MAD LIBS®
SCENE FROM A
HORROR PICTURE

To be read aloud (preferably by live people):

Actor #1: Why did we have to come to this _____ old castle? This
ADJECTIVE

place sends shivers up and down my _____.
PART OF THE BODY

Actor #2: We had no choice. You know all the _____ in town were
PLURAL NOUN

filled because of the _____ convention.
NOUN

Actor #1: I'd have been happy to stay in a/an _____ motel.
ADJECTIVE

Actor #2: Relax. Here comes the bellboy for our _____.
PLURAL NOUN

Actor #1: _____! Look, he's all bent over and has a big
EXCLAMATION

_____ riding on his _____. He looks just like
NOUN   PART OF THE BODY

_____ from that horror flick, *Frankenstein*.
PERSON IN ROOM

Actor #2: No. I think he's my old _____ teacher.
NOUN

Actor #1: I'm putting my _____ down! I'm not staying in this
PART OF THE BODY

_____ place. I'd rather _____ in the car!
ADJECTIVE   VERB

Actor #2: You're worrying _____.
ADVERB

Actor #1: Really? Look at the bellboy. He has my _____ in one hand,
NOUN

your _____ in the other, and his third hand . . . His *third* hand?
NOUN

Ahhhhh!

IN THE GOOD
OLD SUMMERTIME

_____ PLURAL NOUN

_____ PLURAL NOUN

_____ ADVERB

_____ VERB ENDING IN "ING"

_____ ADJECTIVE

_____ NUMBER

_____ PART OF THE BODY

_____ PLURAL NOUN

_____ NOUN

_____ PLURAL NOUN

_____ TYPE OF LIQUID

_____ NOUN

_____ ADVERB

_____ PLURAL NOUN

_____ PLURAL NOUN

_____ NOUN

_____ NOUN

_____ NOUN

_____ NOUN

MAD LIBS®
IN THE GOOD
OLD SUMMERTIME

Many selective _____ prefer the Summer Olympics to the Winter
                     PLURAL NOUN

_____. They respond _____ to such swimming and
PLURAL NOUN   ADVERB

_____ competitions as the hundred-meter _____
VERB ENDING IN "ING"   ADJECTIVE

-style race, the _____-meter _____-stroke race, and, of
                     NUMBER   PART OF THE BODY

course, the diving contests in which _____ dive off a high
                                        PLURAL NOUN

_____ and do triple _____ in the air before landing in
    NOUN   PLURAL NOUN

the _____. Equally fascinating are the track and _____
      TYPE OF LIQUID   NOUN

events in which _____ conditioned _____ compete for
                    ADVERB   PLURAL NOUN

gold _____. They compete in such exciting events as the 1,500-
         PLURAL NOUN

_____ race, the hundred-_____ dash, the ever-popular
      NOUN   NOUN

_____ vaulting, and, last but not least, throwing the hammer, the
      NOUN

javelin, and the _____.
                     NOUN

GOOD MANNERS

NOUN _____

NOUN _____

NOUN _____

VERB _____

PART OF THE BODY _____

ADVERB _____

NOUN _____

NOUN _____

NOUN _____

PART OF THE BODY (PLURAL) _____

NOUN _____

ADJECTIVE _____

ADVERB _____

MAD LIBS®

GOOD MANNERS

1. When you receive a birthday _____ or a wedding _____,
   <u>NOUN</u>   <u>NOUN</u>

   you should always send a thank-you _____.
                                         <u>NOUN</u>

2. When you _____ or burp out loud, be sure to cover your
                  <u>VERB</u>

   _____ and say, "I'm _____ sorry."
   <u>PART OF THE BODY</u>   <u>ADVERB</u>

3. If you are a man and wearing a/an _____ on your head and a/an
                                   <u>NOUN</u>

   _____ approaches, it's always polite to tip your _____.
   <u>NOUN</u>   <u>NOUN</u>

4. When you are at a friend's _____ for dinner, remember, it's not
                            <u>NOUN</u>

   polite to eat with your _____, take food from
                          <u>PART OF THE BODY (PLURAL)</u>

   anyone else's _____, or leave the table before everyone else.
                 <u>NOUN</u>

5. When meeting your friend's parents, always try to make a/an _____
                                                       <u>ADJECTIVE</u>

   impression by greeting them _____.
                                   <u>ADVERB</u>

From GRAB BAG MAD LIBS® • Copyright © 1996, 2001 by Price Stern Sloan,
an imprint of Penguin Group (USA) LLC, 345 Hudson Street, New York, NY 10014.

MAD LIBS® is fun to play with friends, but you can also play it by yourself! To begin with, DO NOT look at the story on the page below. Fill in the blanks on this page with the words called for. Then, using the words you have selected, fill in the blank spaces in the story.

Now you've created your own hilarious MAD LIBS® game!

TV GUIDANCE
PICK OF THE WEEK

NOUN _____

ADJECTIVE _____

NUMBER _____

PLURAL NOUN _____

PLURAL NOUN _____

NOUN _____

PART OF THE BODY (PLURAL) _____

ADJECTIVE _____

PERSON IN ROOM (FEMALE) _____

NOUN _____

PART OF THE BODY _____

PLURAL NOUN _____

ADJECTIVE _____

ADJECTIVE _____

PERSON IN ROOM _____

NOUN _____

NOUN _____

MAD LIBS®
TV GUIDANCE
PICK OF THE WEEK

THURSDAY, 8:00 P.M. *My Adventures as a Foreign* _____.

NOUN

This is an exciting and _____ made-for-TV movie that takes

ADJECTIVE

place during the time of World War _____. We give it a rating of

NUMBER

three _____.

PLURAL NOUN

FRIDAY, 7:30 P.M. *Happy* _____.

PLURAL NOUN

When an old high-school _____ welcomes him with open

NOUN

_____ and throws him a/an _____ party, this

PART OF THE BODY (PLURAL)   ADJECTIVE

puts _____, his former _____ friend, into a bad

PERSON IN ROOM (FEMALE)   NOUN

state of _____.

PART OF THE BODY

SATURDAY, 10:00 P.M. *Where Have All the* _____ *Gone?* This

PLURAL NOUN

_____ thriller, by the _____ director

ADJECTIVE   ADJECTIVE

_____, is about a Manhattan _____ searching for a

PERSON IN ROOM   NOUN

missing person in a small _____.

NOUN

MAD LIBS® is fun to play with friends, but you can also play it by yourself! To begin with, DO NOT look at the story on the page below. Fill in the blanks on this page with the words called for. Then, using the words you have selected, fill in the blank spaces in the story.

Now you've created your own hilarious MAD LIBS® game!

GOOD HEALTH TO ONE AND ALL

_____ ADJECTIVE

_____ ADJECTIVE

_____ VERB ENDING IN "ING"

_____ PART OF THE BODY (PLURAL)

_____ PLURAL NOUN

_____ PLURAL NOUN

_____ NOUN

_____ PLURAL NOUN

_____ PLURAL NOUN

_____ NOUN

_____ PLURAL NOUN

_____ PLURAL NOUN

_____ ADJECTIVE

_____ PLURAL NOUN

_____ ADJECTIVE

_____ ADJECTIVE

MAD LIBS®
GOOD HEALTH
TO ONE AND ALL

A/An _____ fitness revolution is taking place. Today, millions of
        ADJECTIVE

people are doing all kinds of _____ exercises such as jogging,
                            ADJECTIVE

walking, and _____ to get their _____
            VERB ENDING IN "ING"   PART OF THE BODY (PLURAL)

in shape and develop their _____. Many go to gyms and health
                          PLURAL NOUN

_____ to work out by punching a/an _____, lifting
PLURAL NOUN   NOUN

_____, or performing aerobic _____. In the past
PLURAL NOUN   PLURAL NOUN

_____ people have become very weight conscious. They have
NOUN

learned what _____ they should and should not eat. They know it's
            PLURAL NOUN

healthy to eat green _____ and _____ fruit. They also
                    PLURAL NOUN   ADJECTIVE

know to avoid foods high in _____ and _____ fats,
                           PLURAL NOUN   ADJECTIVE

especially if they want to lead a long and _____ life.
                                          ADJECTIVE

MAD LIBS® is fun to play with friends, but you can also play it by yourself! To begin with, DO NOT look at the story on the page below. Fill in the blanks on this page with the words called for. Then, using the words you have selected, fill in the blank spaces in the story.

Now you've created your own hilarious MAD LIBS® game!

WHY DO SKUNKS SMELL?

_____ NOUN

_____ ADJECTIVE

_____ PLURAL NOUN

_____ A PLACE

_____ PLURAL NOUN

_____ ADJECTIVE

_____ NOUN

_____ VERB ENDING IN "ING"

_____ PART OF THE BODY

_____ PART OF THE BODY (PLURAL)

_____ PART OF THE BODY (PLURAL)

_____ ADVERB

_____ COLOR

_____ PART OF THE BODY

_____ PART OF THE BODY

MAD LIBS®

WHY DO SKUNKS SMELL?

Surprisingly, a skunk is a friendly _____ who can make a/an
                                        NOUN

_____ household pet. But what makes these _____
   ADJECTIVE   PLURAL NOUN

smell to high (the) _____? The skunk has scent _____
                        A PLACE   PLURAL NOUN

that contain a/an _____-smelling fluid. When attacked, the
                      ADJECTIVE

skunk aims this smelly _____ at its enemies. But the skunk does
                            NOUN

give warning before _____. It raises its _____
                       VERB ENDING IN "ING"   PART OF THE BODY

first, or stamps its _____ so that you can run away as fast
                       PART OF THE BODY (PLURAL)

as your _____ can carry you. The most _____
           PART OF THE BODY (PLURAL)   ADVERB

recognizable skunk is the one with a _____ line on its _____
                                        COLOR   PART OF THE BODY

and another one between its _____ and its ears.
                               PART OF THE BODY

FAMOUS QUOTES FROM THE AMERICAN REVOLUTION

NOUN _____

NOUN _____

COLOR _____

PART OF THE BODY (PLURAL) _____

NOUN _____

PLURAL NOUN _____

VERB ENDING IN "ING" _____

NOUN _____

PLURAL NOUN _____

PLURAL NOUN _____

ADJECTIVE _____

NOUN _____

Now you've created your own hilarious MAD LIBS® game!

MAD LIBS® is fun to play with friends, but you can also play it by yourself! To begin with, DO NOT look at the story on the page below. Fill in the blanks on this page with the words called for. Then, using the words you have selected, fill in the blank spaces in the story.

MAD LIBS®
FAMOUS QUOTES FROM
THE AMERICAN REVOLUTION

Nathan Hale said: "I regret that I have but one _____ to give for
                                                    NOUN

my _____."
         NOUN

William Prescott said: "Don't fire until you see the _____ of their
                                                          COLOR

_____."
PART OF THE BODY (PLURAL)

Patrick Henry said: "Give me liberty or give me _____."
                                                        NOUN

Paul Revere said: "The _____ are _____."
                           PLURAL NOUN   VERB ENDING IN "ING"

John Hancock said: "I wrote my _____ large so the king could
                                      NOUN

read it without his _____."
                          PLURAL NOUN

Thomas Jefferson said: "All _____ are created equal. They are
                                  PLURAL NOUN

endowed by their creator with certain _____ rights and among
                                              ADJECTIVE

these are life, liberty, and the pursuit of _____."
                                                  NOUN

From GRAB BAG MAD LIBS® • Copyright © 1996, 2001 by Price Stern Sloan,
an imprint of Penguin Group (USA) LLC, 345 Hudson Street, New York, NY 10014.

MADLIBS®

SLEEPOVER PARTY
MAD LIBS

by Roger Price & Leonard Stern

PSS!

PRICE STERN SLOAN

An Imprint of Penguin Group (USA) LLC

INSTRUCTIONS

MAD LIBS® is a game for people who don't like games!
It can be played by one, two, three, four, or forty.

• RIDICULOUSLY SIMPLE DIRECTIONS

In this tablet you will find stories containing blank spaces where words are left out. One player, the READER, selects one of these stories. The READER does not tell anyone what the story is about. Instead, he/she asks the other players, the WRITERS, to give him/her words. These words are used to fill in the blank spaces in the story.

• TO PLAY

The READER asks each WRITER in turn to call out a word—an adjective or a noun or whatever the space calls for—and uses them to fill in the blank spaces in the story. The result is a MAD LIBS® game.

When the READER then reads the completed MAD LIBS® game to the other players, they will discover that they have written a story that is fantastic, screamingly funny, shocking, silly, crazy, or just plain dumb—depending upon which words each WRITER called out.

• EXAMPLE (*Before* and *After*)

"_____!" he said _____
    EXCLAMATION   ADVERB

as he jumped into his convertible _____ and
                                      NOUN

drove off with his _____ wife.
                 ADJECTIVE

"_____*Ouch*_____!" he said _____*stupidly*_____
    EXCLAMATION   ADVERB

as he jumped into his convertible _____*cat*_____ and
                                      NOUN

drove off with his _____*brave*_____ wife.
                 ADJECTIVE

QUICK REVIEW

In case you have forgotten what adjectives, adverbs, nouns, and verbs are, here is a quick review:

An ADJECTIVE describes something or somebody. *Lumpy, soft, ugly, messy,* and *short* are adjectives.

An ADVERB tells how something is done. It modifies a verb and usually ends in "ly." *Modestly, stupidly, greedily,* and *carefully* are adverbs.

A NOUN is the name of a person, place, or thing. *Sidewalk, umbrella, bridle, bathtub,* and *nose* are nouns.

A VERB is an action word. *Run, pitch, jump,* and *swim* are verbs. Put the verbs in past tense if the directions say PAST TENSE. *Ran, pitched, jumped,* and *swam* are verbs in the past tense.

When we ask for A PLACE, we mean any sort of place: a country or city *(Spain, Cleveland)* or a room *(bathroom, kitchen).*

An EXCLAMATION or SILLY WORD is any sort of funny sound, gasp, grunt, or outcry, like *Wow!, Ouch!, Whomp!, Ick!,* and *Gadzooks!*

When we ask for specific words, like a NUMBER, a COLOR, an ANIMAL, or a PART OF THE BODY, we mean a word that is one of those things, like *seven, blue, horse,* or *head.*

When we ask for a PLURAL, it means more than one. For example, *cat* pluralized is *cats.*

MAD LIBS® is fun to play with friends, but you can also play it by yourself! To begin with, DO NOT look at the story on the page below. Fill in the blanks on this page with the words called for. Then, using the words you have selected, fill in the blank spaces in the story.

Now you've created your own hilarious MAD LIBS® game!

YOU'RE INVITED

PERSON IN ROOM (FEMALE) _____

ADJECTIVE _____

NOUN _____

NOUN _____

CELEBRITY _____

ADVERB _____

NUMBER _____

ADJECTIVE _____

NOUN _____

NOUN _____

PART OF THE BODY _____

PLURAL NOUN _____

ADJECTIVE _____

PLURAL NOUN _____

PLURAL NOUN _____

ADJECTIVE _____

PLURAL NOUN _____

LETTER OF THE ALPHABET _____

CELEBRITY _____

SAME CELEBRITY _____

ADJECTIVE _____

MAD LIBS®

YOU'RE INVITED

Dear _____,
<u>PERSON IN ROOM (FEMALE)</u>

I would like to invite you to a/an _____ sleepover party this Friday
<u>ADJECTIVE</u>

night at my _____. I live on the corner of South _____ Street
<u>NOUN</u>   <u>NOUN</u>

and _____ Lane. Please arrive _____ at _____ o'clock.
<u>CELEBRITY</u>   <u>ADVERB</u>   <u>NUMBER</u>

Don't forget to bring a/an _____ sleeping _____ and a
<u>ADJECTIVE</u>   <u>NOUN</u>

soft _____ to rest your _____ on. We'll have pizza
<u>NOUN</u>   <u>PART OF THE BODY</u>

topped with _____ for dinner, and we'll watch a/an
<u>PLURAL NOUN</u>

_____ movie. When it is time for bed, we'll all change into our
<u>ADJECTIVE</u>

_____ and turn out the _____. Then we'll tell
<u>PLURAL NOUN</u>   <u>PLURAL NOUN</u>

_____ ghost stories and talk about all the cute _____ at
<u>ADJECTIVE</u>   <u>PLURAL NOUN</u>

school! Please RSV-_____ to me by e-mail at iluv-
<u>LETTER OF THE ALPHABET</u>

_____@_____.com. Hope you can join our _____
<u>CELEBRITY</u>   <u>SAME CELEBRITY</u>   <u>ADJECTIVE</u>

party!

MAD LIBS' is fun to play with friends, but you can also play it by yourself! To begin with, DO NOT look at the story on the page below. Fill in the blanks on this page with the words called for. Then, using the words you have selected, fill in the blank spaces in the story.

Now you've created your own hilarious MAD LIBS' game!

LET'S GET PACKING!

NOUN _____

ADJECTIVE _____

NOUN _____

ADJECTIVE _____

PLURAL NOUN _____

NOUN _____

PART OF THE BODY (PLURAL) _____

VERB _____

ADJECTIVE _____

CELEBRITY _____

VERB _____

ADVERB _____

ADJECTIVE _____

NOUN _____

VERB _____

VERB ENDING IN "ING" _____

NOUN _____

ADJECTIVE _____

MAD LIBS®

LET'S GET PACKING!

If you are going to a sleepover at a friend's _____, here's a/an
                                                    NOUN

_____ list of things to put in your overnight _____:
     ADJECTIVE   NOUN

1. _____ pajamas and a change of _____ for the next day.
        ADJECTIVE   PLURAL NOUN

2. A tooth-_____ for brushing your _____.
              NOUN   PART OF THE BODY (PLURAL)

3. Some CDs so you and your friends can _____ to your favorite
                                              VERB

_____ tunes.
     ADJECTIVE

4. Magazines with someone like _____ on the cover and articles
                                    CELEBRITY

about how to _____ _____.
                  VERB   ADVERB

5. A/An _____ _____-light will help you to
              ADJECTIVE   NOUN

_____ in the dark while you stay up _____
      VERB   VERB ENDING IN "ING"

into the wee hours of the _____.
                               NOUN

If you follow this checklist, you should have a really _____
                                                            ADJECTIVE

sleepover.

PILLOW FIGHT!

ADJECTIVE _____

PERSON IN ROOM (FEMALE) _____

ADJECTIVE _____

NOUN _____

PART OF THE BODY _____

NOUN _____

PERSON IN ROOM (FEMALE) _____

PART OF THE BODY (PLURAL) _____

NOUN _____

PLURAL NOUN _____

ADJECTIVE _____

ADJECTIVE _____

ADJECTIVE _____

Now you've created your own hilarious MAD LIBS® game!

MAD LIBS® is fun to play with friends, but you can also play it by yourself! To begin with, DO NOT look at the story on the page below. Fill in the blanks on this page with the words called for. Then, using the words you have selected, fill in the blank spaces in the story.

MAD LIBS®

PILLOW FIGHT!

The last time I went to a sleepover, a/an _____ pillow fight broke
                                                    ADJECTIVE

out. Out of nowhere, _____ grabbed her
                              PERSON IN ROOM (FEMALE)

_____, fluffy _____ and began swinging it at anyone
     ADJECTIVE   NOUN

close to her. Soon, everyone else joined in! At one point, I got hit right in the

back of my _____. As soon as I recovered, I tossed my
                 PART OF THE BODY

_____ at _____'s _____, but I
     NOUN   PERSON IN ROOM (FEMALE)   PART OF THE BODY (PLURAL)

missed. Instead, I knocked over an expensive _____ and my pillow
                                                       NOUN

split open! _____ flew everywhere, covering the room in a layer of
              PLURAL NOUN

_____ feathers. The fighting stopped when we all broke out in
  ADJECTIVE

_____ laughter. The fun ended when we realized we had to clean up
  ADJECTIVE

the _____ mess!
       ADJECTIVE

MAD LIBS® is fun to play with friends, but you can also play it by yourself! To begin with, DO NOT look at the story on the page below. Fill in the blanks on this page with the words called for. Then, using the words you have selected, fill in the blank spaces in the story.

Now you've created your own hilarious MAD LIBS® game!

SLEEPWALKING

VERB ENDING IN "ING" _____

ADJECTIVE _____

PLURAL NOUN _____

PLURAL NOUN _____

VERB _____

PART OF THE BODY (PLURAL) _____

VERB _____

ADJECTIVE _____

NOUN _____

NOUN _____

PLURAL NOUN _____

ADJECTIVE _____

NOUN _____

SILLY WORD _____

PLURAL NOUN _____

MAD LIBS

SLEEPWALKING

Sleep-_____ is a/an _____ phenomenon that a
        VERB ENDING IN "ING"   ADJECTIVE

surprising number of _____ experience. Usually, sleepwalkers climb
                        PLURAL NOUN

out of their _____ and begin to _____ with their
                PLURAL NOUN   VERB

_____ tightly shut. Sometimes they _____
PART OF THE BODY (PLURAL)   VERB

outdoors wearing only their _____ pajamas. And it's not
                                  ADJECTIVE

uncommon for _____-walkers to raid the _____ and eat lots
                  NOUN   NOUN

of _____. What's truly amazing is that they don't remember a/an
      PLURAL NOUN

_____ thing the following _____. They'll open the fridge
    ADJECTIVE   NOUN

and say, "_____! Where did all the _____ go?" They may
            SILLY WORD   PLURAL NOUN

never know!

MAD LIBS' is fun to play with friends, but you can also play it by yourself! To begin with, DO NOT look at the story on the page below. Fill in the blanks on this page with the words called for. Then, using the words you have selected, fill in the blank spaces in the story.

Now you've created your own hilarious MAD LIBS' game!

M.A.S.H.

_____ ADJECTIVE

_____ NUMBER

_____ PLURAL NOUN

_____ A PLACE

_____ PERSON IN ROOM (MALE)

_____ ADJECTIVE

_____ A PLACE

_____ ADJECTIVE

_____ ADJECTIVE

_____ NOUN

_____ A PLACE

_____ ADJECTIVE

_____ NUMBER

_____ NOUN

_____ NUMBER

_____ OCCUPATION

_____ NOUN

_____ ADJECTIVE

MAD LIBS®

M.A.S.H.

Congratulations! According to M.A.S.H. (the ultimate sleepover game), your

future looks bright and _____. When you are _____ years
                          ADJECTIVE   NUMBER

old, you will meet the man of your _____ at (the)
                                        PLURAL NOUN

_____. His name will be _____. You will have a/an
   A PLACE   PERSON IN ROOM (MALE)

_____ wedding, and you will go to (the) _____ on
   ADJECTIVE   A PLACE

your _____ honeymoon. When you return, you will move into a/an
         ADJECTIVE

_____ _____ in (the) _____. You will drive
   ADJECTIVE   NOUN   A PLACE

a/an _____ car. Then, when you have been married for _____
         ADJECTIVE   NUMBER

years, you will have your first _____. You will go on to have
                                     NOUN

_____ more children. You will work as a/an _____ until you
   NUMBER   OCCUPATION

retire and move to a tropical _____. Your M.A.S.H. future
                                     NOUN

looks prosperous and _____, so prepare to enjoy it!
                          ADJECTIVE

MAD LIBS® is fun to play with friends, but you can also play it by yourself! To begin with, DO NOT look at the story on the page below. Fill in the blanks on this page with the words called for. Then, using the words you have selected, fill in the blank spaces in the story.

Now you've created your own hilarious MAD LIBS® game!

PRANKS FOR NOTHING

ADJECTIVE _____

ADJECTIVE _____

PLURAL NOUN _____

ADJECTIVE _____

PLURAL NOUN _____

PLURAL NOUN _____

ADJECTIVE _____

VERB ENDING IN "ING" _____

NOUN _____

NOUN _____

ADJECTIVE _____

NOUN _____

ADJECTIVE _____

PART OF THE BODY _____

ADJECTIVE _____

PLURAL NOUN _____

PART OF THE BODY (PLURAL) _____

ADJECTIVE _____

PART OF THE BODY (PLURAL) _____

COLOR _____

MAD LIBS

PRANKS FOR NOTHING

Whenever my _____ sister and her _____
                    ADJECTIVE   ADJECTIVE

_____ have a sleepover party, I love to play _____ pranks
  PLURAL NOUN   ADJECTIVE

on them. Once, I put gummy _____ in everyone's sleeping
                               PLURAL NOUN

_____. They thought they were _____ bugs, and they
  PLURAL NOUN   ADJECTIVE

were out of their _____ bags in record time! Another time, I hid
                  VERB ENDING IN "ING"

all the rolls of _____ paper in the trunk of Dad's _____,
                    NOUN   NOUN

not knowing that Dad, a/an _____ doctor, was on duty at the
                              ADJECTIVE

_____ that night. But the most _____ prank of all time
     NOUN   ADJECTIVE

was when I replaced all of the _____-paste with _____
                               PART OF THE BODY   ADJECTIVE

icing. When my sister's _____ brushed their _____
                          PLURAL NOUN   PART OF THE BODY (PLURAL)

with it, the _____ looks on their _____ were
                ADJECTIVE   PART OF THE BODY (PLURAL)

priceless—but the _____ icing all over their teeth was even better!
                      COLOR

From SLEEPOVER PARTY MAD LIBS® • Copyright © 2008 by Price Stern Sloan,
an imprint of Penguin Group (USA) LLC, 345 Hudson Street, New York, NY 10014.

LIGHT AS A FEATHER

_____ ADJECTIVE

_____ ADJECTIVE

_____ ADJECTIVE

_____ ADJECTIVE

_____ NOUN

_____ PLURAL NOUN

_____ PART OF THE BODY (PLURAL)

_____ ADVERB

_____ ADJECTIVE

_____ NUMBER

_____ NOUN

_____ NOUN

_____ NOUN

_____ ADVERB

_____ NOUN

_____ NOUN

_____ ADVERB

_____ PLURAL NOUN

_____ ADJECTIVE

MAD LIBS® is fun to play with friends, but you can also play it by yourself! To begin with, DO NOT look at the story on the page below. Fill in the blanks on this page with the words called for. Then, using the words you have selected, fill in the blank spaces in the story.

Now you've created your own hilarious MAD LIBS® game!

MAD LIBS®

LIGHT AS A FEATHER

Another _____ sleepover game is _____ as a feather,
          ADJECTIVE   ADJECTIVE

_____ as a board. You'll need a/an _____ volunteer to
    ADJECTIVE   ADJECTIVE

lie down on the _____ with her _____ closed and her
                      NOUN   PLURAL NOUN

_____ folded across her chest. Tell her to breathe
  PART OF THE BODY (PLURAL)

_____ and remain _____ and relaxed. Then gather in a
     ADVERB   ADJECTIVE

circle around her, placing _____ fingers underneath her _____
                                 NUMBER   NOUN

as you repeat the phrase, "Light as a/an _____, stiff as a/an
                                               NOUN

_____." On the count of three, _____ lift her off the
     NOUN   ADVERB

_____ and raise her to the _____. Then lower her down
     NOUN   NOUN

_____. Your _____ will be completely amazed at this
     ADVERB   PLURAL NOUN

_____feat!
   ADJECTIVE

MAD LIBS® is fun to play with friends, but you can also play it by yourself! To begin with, DO NOT look at the story on the page below. Fill in the blanks on this page with the words called for. Then, using the words you have selected, fill in the blank spaces in the story.

Now you've created your own hilarious MAD LIBS® game!

LET'S DANCE!

_____
ADJECTIVE

_____
PLURAL NOUN

_____
NUMBER

_____
PLURAL NOUN

_____
ADJECTIVE

_____
ADVERB

_____
ADJECTIVE

_____
NOUN

_____
VERB (PAST TENSE)

_____
PART OF THE BODY

_____
PERSON IN ROOM

_____
ADJECTIVE

_____
NUMBER

_____
PART OF THE BODY

_____
ADVERB

_____
ADJECTIVE

_____
PLURAL NOUN

_____
ADVERB

_____
PLURAL NOUN

_____
NOUN

_____
PART OF THE BODY (PLURAL)

MAD LIBS

LET'S DANCE!

At my _____ sleepover party, my best _____ and I
       ADJECTIVE   PLURAL NOUN

decided to have a dance-off. We made my _____-year-old little sister be
                                       NUMBER

the judge. We broke into two teams, "The _____" and "The
                                   PLURAL NOUN

_____ Dancers." My team danced _____, but the other
ADJECTIVE   ADVERB

team's _____ moves were out of this _____! They totally
        ADJECTIVE   NOUN

out-_____ us. So when no one was looking, I grabbed my sister
   VERB (PAST TENSE)

by the _____ and pulled her aside. "_____," I whispered,
   PART OF THE BODY   PERSON IN ROOM

"I promise to do all of your _____ chores for _____ months
                          ADJECTIVE   NUMBER

if you say that my team won." My sister shook her _____. "No
                                        PART OF THE BODY

way!" she said _____. "Your team danced worse than a bunch of
             ADVERB

_____-_____!" "Fine," I said. "Then I'll just have to tell
ADJECTIVE   PLURAL NOUN

all of my friends that you're _____ afraid of _____."
                          ADVERB   PLURAL NOUN

That helped to change her _____. We won that contest,
                         NOUN

_____ down!
PART OF THE BODY (PLURAL)

SNORE NO MORE

ADJECTIVE _____

NOUN _____

NOUN _____

ADJECTIVE _____

VERB ENDING IN "ING" _____

VERB _____

PART OF THE BODY _____

VERB ENDING IN "ING" _____

ADJECTIVE _____

ADJECTIVE _____

ADJECTIVE _____

VERB ENDING IN "ING" _____

ADJECTIVE _____

ADJECTIVE _____

PART OF THE BODY _____

MAD LIBS®

SNORE NO MORE

Snoring is a loud and often _____ sound that can be compared to
ADJECTIVE

sawing a piece of _____ or to a freight _____ roaring down
NOUN   NOUN

the tracks. Fortunately, there are many _____ solutions to keep a
ADJECTIVE

snorer from _____:
VERB ENDING IN "ING"

1. _____ on your _____ instead of on your back.
VERB   PART OF THE BODY

2. Try _____ without a/an _____ pillow.
VERB ENDING IN "ING"   ADJECTIVE

3. Learn to play the didgeridoo, a/an _____ Australian wind
ADJECTIVE

instrument. Studies have shown that this strengthens _____
ADJECTIVE

airways and helps reduce _____. The trouble with this
VERB ENDING IN "ING"

_____ solution is that most people can't stand the
ADJECTIVE

_____ sound of the didgeridoo.
ADJECTIVE

4. If all else fails and the snoring continues, buy a pair of _____-
PART OF THE BODY

plugs for anyone sleeping nearby!

PIZZA PARTY

CELEBRITY _____

ADJECTIVE _____

NUMBER _____

ADJECTIVE _____

PLURAL NOUN _____

PLURAL NOUN _____

NOUN _____

ADJECTIVE _____

PLURAL NOUN _____

PLURAL NOUN _____

ADJECTIVE _____

PLURAL NOUN _____

PLURAL NOUN _____

NOUN _____

MAD LIBS® is fun to play with friends, but you can also play it by yourself! To begin with, DO NOT look at the story on the page below. Fill in the blanks on this page with the words called for. Then, using the words you have selected, fill in the blank spaces in the story.

Now you've created your own hilarious MAD LIBS® game!

MAD LIBS

PIZZA PARTY

CLERK: Hello, _____'s Pizza Shop. How can I help you?
                        CELEBRITY

GIRL: I'm having a/an _____ party, and I would like to order
                              ADJECTIVE

enough pizza for _____ _____ people.
                    NUMBER   ADJECTIVE

CLERK: Five large _____ should be enough. What
                          PLURAL NOUN

_____ would you like on them? Tonight's special is pizza topped with
   PLURAL NOUN

_____ cheese, _____ tomatoes, and green _____.
      NOUN   ADJECTIVE   PLURAL NOUN

GIRL: Can you add sliced _____ and _____ onions, too?
                                 PLURAL NOUN   ADJECTIVE

CLERK: Can do. Since you're ordering more than fifty _____,
                                                            PLURAL NOUN

worth of food, you get free _____ for dessert.
                                 PLURAL NOUN

GIRL: Thanks. And please hurry. We're so hungry, we could eat a/an

_____!
      NOUN

MAD LIBS® is fun to play with friends, but you can also play it by yourself! To begin with, DO NOT look at the story on the page below. Fill in the blanks on this page with the words called for. Then, using the words you have selected, fill in the blank spaces in the story.

Now you've created your own hilarious MAD LIBS® game!

NO BOYS ALLOWED!

PERSON IN ROOM (MALE) _____

ADJECTIVE _____

NOUN _____

PLURAL NOUN _____

ADJECTIVE _____

ADJECTIVE _____

ADJECTIVE _____

PART OF THE BODY _____

PLURAL NOUN _____

PART OF THE BODY (PLURAL) _____

PLURAL NOUN _____

MAD LIBS®

NO BOYS ALLOWED!

Attention, _____! _____ boys are NOT allowed to
        PERSON IN ROOM (MALE)   ADJECTIVE

enter this room. This ESPECIALLY goes for _____-faced brothers like
        NOUN

you! There is a/an _____-only _____ party in progress,
        PLURAL NOUN   ADJECTIVE

and you are not invited. If you dare enter, be aware that you are a target for

_____ pranks. We may even subject you to a/an _____
  ADJECTIVE   ADJECTIVE

makeover and put makeup on your _____ before we let you
        PART OF THE BODY

escape. So, if you are made of _____ and snails and puppy-dog
        PLURAL NOUN

_____, please go back to where you came from. No
  PART OF THE BODY (PLURAL)

_____ allowed!
  PLURAL NOUN

MAD LIBS® is fun to play with friends, but you can also play it by yourself! To begin with, DO NOT look at the story on the page below. Fill in the blanks on this page with the words called for. Then, using the words you have selected, fill in the blank spaces in the story.

Now you've created your own hilarious MAD LIBS® game!

MIDNIGHT MOVIES

ADJECTIVE _____

ADJECTIVE _____

PERSON IN ROOM (FEMALE) _____

NOUN _____

ADJECTIVE _____

NOUN _____

PLURAL NOUN _____

ADJECTIVE _____

ADJECTIVE _____

NOUN _____

NOUN _____

PART OF THE BODY _____

PLURAL NOUN _____

PERSON IN ROOM (FEMALE) _____

NOUN _____

NOUN _____

ADJECTIVE _____

NOUN _____

MAD LIBS®

MIDNIGHT MOVIES

Looking for the perfect movie to watch at your sleepover? Try one of these

_____ party favorites:
   ADJECTIVE

- _____ *Girls*: This film stars _____ Lohan as a
  ADJECTIVE   PERSON IN ROOM (FEMALE)

homeschooled _____ who goes to a/an _____ high
          NOUN   ADJECTIVE

school for the first time. Will she turn into a mean _____ like the
                                   NOUN

rest of the popular _____?
            PLURAL NOUN

- *Legally* _____: In this movie, a/an _____ sorority
        ADJECTIVE   ADJECTIVE

_____ follows her ex-boyfriend to an Ivy _____ school in
    NOUN   NOUN

an attempt to win back his _____.
                  PART OF THE BODY

- *The Princess* _____: When _____ Thermopolis
          PLURAL NOUN   PERSON IN ROOM (FEMALE)

discovers she is a/an _____ and an heir to the _____ of a/
            NOUN   NOUN

an _____ country, her entire _____ is turned upside down.
  ADJECTIVE   NOUN

MAD LIBS® is fun to play with friends, but you can also play it by yourself! To begin with, DO NOT look at the story on the page below. Fill in the blanks on this page with the words called for. Then, using the words you have selected, fill in the blank spaces in the story.

Now you've created your own hilarious MAD LIBS® game!

A GHASTLY GHOST STORY (PART 1)

ADJECTIVE _____

PLURAL NOUN _____

NOUN _____

NOUN _____

ADJECTIVE _____

PLURAL NOUN _____

NOUN _____

VERB (PAST TENSE) _____

ADJECTIVE _____

NOUN _____

ADJECTIVE _____

PART OF THE BODY (PLURAL) _____

MAD LIBS

A GHASTLY GHOST STORY
(PART 1)

One dark and _____ night I had a sleepover party with seven
                    ADJECTIVE

_____ at my family's old Victorian _____ at the edge of
   PLURAL NOUN   NOUN

town. I was the first person in the house to fall asleep, and in the middle of the

_____, I was startled awake by a/an _____ sound coming
     NOUN   ADJECTIVE

from the attic. I couldn't stop my _____ from shaking as I slipped into
                                       PLURAL NOUN

a/an _____, _____ upstairs, and opened the door to
        NOUN   VERB (PAST TENSE)

the attic. Out of nowhere, a/an _____ figure in a pale white
                                      ADJECTIVE

_____ with long _____ hair flew past me. Terrified, I
     NOUN   ADJECTIVE

screamed at the top of my _____.
                             PART OF THE BODY (PLURAL)

MAD LIBS® is fun to play with friends, but you can also play it by yourself! To begin with, DO NOT look at the story on the page below. Fill in the blanks on this page with the words called for. Then, using the words you have selected, fill in the blank spaces in the story.

Now you've created your own hilarious MAD LIBS® game!

A GHASTLY GHOST STORY (PART 2)

NOUN _____

VERB ENDING IN "ING" _____

NOUN _____

PLURAL NOUN _____

NOUN _____

PART OF THE BODY _____

PLURAL NOUN _____

PLURAL NOUN _____

ADJECTIVE _____

ADJECTIVE _____

ADVERB _____

NOUN _____

NOUN _____

MAD LIBS®
A GHASTLY GHOST STORY
(PART 2)

"Relax," said the _____. "You're _____ like a leaf,
                    NOUN   VERB ENDING IN "ING"

but you need not be afraid. I am a friendly _____." "Really?"
                                              NOUN

I said. "Wow! I can't wait for you to meet my _____."
                                               PLURAL NOUN

"I would love to, but unfortunately I can only reveal myself to the first

_____ who falls asleep," the ghost replied. And in the blink of a/an
   NOUN

_____, the ghost was gone. I ran to awaken my sleeping
  PART OF THE BODY

_____ to tell them what had happened, but they said they didn't
  PLURAL NOUN

believe me. They told me I'd lost all my _____! But I could tell they
                                          PLURAL NOUN

wished they had seen the _____ ghost. Sure enough, the next time I
                           ADJECTIVE

had a sleepover at my _____ house, each girl tried _____
                        ADJECTIVE   ADVERB

to be the first _____ to fall asleep and meet the friendly
                  NOUN

_____!
   NOUN

MAD LIBS® is fun to play with friends, but you can also play it by
yourself! To begin with, DO NOT look at the story on the page
below. Fill in the blanks on this page with the words called for. Then,
using the words you have selected, fill in the blank spaces in the story.

Now you've created your own hilarious MAD LIBS® game!

HOT FUDGE SUNDAES

NOUN _____

NUMBER _____

PLURAL NOUN _____

ADJECTIVE _____

ADJECTIVE _____

ADJECTIVE _____

NOUN _____

NUMBER _____

PLURAL NOUN _____

NOUN _____

NOUN _____

NOUN _____

VERB (PAST TENSE) _____

PLURAL NOUN _____

ADJECTIVE _____

VERB _____

MAD LIBS®

HOT FUDGE SUNDAES

Making a hot fudge _____ is as simple as one, two, _____. All you
NOUN   NUMBER

need are the following _____:
PLURAL NOUN

   A pint of _____ ice cream
   ADJECTIVE

   1 jar of _____ fudge sauce
   ADJECTIVE

   1 cup of _____ nuts
   ADJECTIVE

   1 can of whipped _____
   NOUN

   _____ maraschino _____
   NUMBER   PLURAL NOUN

Scoop the ice _____ into a glass _____. Pour on a generous
NOUN   NOUN

portion of hot _____ sauce, and add a heaping mound of
NOUN

_____ cream. Sprinkle with _____ and top off with
VERB (PAST TENSE)   PLURAL NOUN

a/an _____ cherry. Now _____ and enjoy!
ADJECTIVE   VERB

TRUTH OR DARE (PART 1)

_____ NOUN

_____ PERSON IN ROOM (MALE)

_____ NOUN

_____ NUMBER

_____ VERB (PAST TENSE)

_____ NOUN

_____ NUMBER

_____ ADJECTIVE

_____ VERB

_____ NOUN

_____ ADJECTIVE

_____ NOUN

_____ ADJECTIVE

_____ TYPE OF LIQUID

_____ NOUN

_____ PLURAL NOUN

_____ TYPE OF LIQUID

MAD LIBS® is fun to play with friends, but you can also play it by yourself! To begin with, DO NOT look at the story on the page below. Fill in the blanks on this page with the words called for. Then, using the words you have selected, fill in the blank spaces in the story.

Now you've created your own hilarious MAD LIBS® game!

MAD LIBS®

TRUTH OR DARE (PART 1)

Let's play truth or dare! First, some truths:

Q: What is the name of the _____ you like?
                              NOUN

A: _____.
   PERSON IN ROOM (MALE)

Q: What is one _____ no one knows about you?
                  NOUN

A: When I was _____ years old, I _____ like a/an
                  NUMBER   VERB (PAST TENSE)

_____ in front of _____ people.
   NOUN   NUMBER

Q: If you were stranded on a/an _____ island, what three things
                                   ADJECTIVE

would you bring with you?

A: I couldn't _____ without my precious _____, my
                 VERB   NOUN

_____ _____, and a/an _____ bottle of
   ADJECTIVE   NOUN   ADJECTIVE

_____.
   TYPE OF LIQUID

Q: What is the strangest _____ you have ever eaten?
                            NOUN

A: _____ dipped in _____.
   PLURAL NOUN   TYPE OF LIQUID

MAD LIBS' is fun to play with friends, but you can also play it by yourself! To begin with, DO NOT look at the story on the page below. Fill in the blanks on this page with the words called for. Then, using the words you have selected, fill in the blank spaces in the story.

Now you've created your own hilarious MAD LIBS' game!

TRUTH OR DARE (PART 2)

_____ ADJECTIVE

_____ VERB

_____ NOUN

_____ ADJECTIVE

_____ ADJECTIVE

_____ NOUN

_____ NOUN

_____ VERB

_____ PLURAL NOUN

_____ ADJECTIVE

_____ PART OF THE BODY (PLURAL)

_____ NUMBER

MAD LIBS®

TRUTH OR DARE (PART 2)

And now for the dares!

DARE: Pretend you are a/an _____ puppy. _____ loudly and
                              ADJECTIVE   VERB

wag your _____ .
              NOUN

DARE: Put on some _____ music and dance like a/an
                          ADJECTIVE

_____ _____ for one minute.
   ADJECTIVE   NOUN

DARE: Hop on one _____ while you _____ and say the
                      NOUN   VERB

alphabet backward.

DARE: Take off your socks and _____ and step into the shower.
                                   PLURAL NOUN

Then turn on the _____ water and yodel at the top of your
                     ADJECTIVE

_____ for _____ seconds.
PART OF THE BODY (PLURAL)   NUMBER

MAD LIBS® is fun to play with friends, but you can also play it by yourself! To begin with, DO NOT look at the story on the page below. Fill in the blanks on this page with the words called for. Then, using the words you have selected, fill in the blank spaces in the story.

Now you've created your own hilarious MAD LIBS® game!

A BAD NIGHTMARE

PERSON IN ROOM (FEMALE) _____

ADJECTIVE _____

PLURAL NOUN _____

NOUN _____

PLURAL NOUN _____

PLURAL NOUN _____

ADVERB _____

PART OF THE BODY (PLURAL) _____

NOUN _____

NOUN _____

SAME NOUN _____

VERB ENDING IN "ING" _____

VERB ENDING IN "ING" _____

MAD LIBS®

A BAD NIGHTMARE

One night when I slept over at my friend _____'s house I had
_{PERSON IN ROOM (FEMALE)}

a/an _____ nightmare that scared the living _____ out of
_{ADJECTIVE} _{PLURAL NOUN}

me. I dreamed I was in school, standing in front of my English _____,
_{NOUN}

giving a report on Shakespeare's _____, when I realized I wasn't
_{PLURAL NOUN}

wearing any _____. Embarrassed beyond belief, I _____
_{PLURAL NOUN} _{ADVERB}

put my hands over my _____ and ran out of the classroom
_{PART OF THE BODY (PLURAL)}

at breakneck _____. Suddenly, I was being chased by a wild
_{NOUN}

_____! Just as the _____ was about to catch me, I woke up
_{NOUN} _{SAME NOUN}

_____ with fright. I spent the rest of the night _____
_{VERB ENDING IN "ING"} _{VERB ENDING IN "ING"}

with the light on!

From SLEEPOVER PARTY MAD LIBS® • Copyright © 2008 by Price Stern Sloan,
an imprint of Penguin Group (USA) LLC, 345 Hudson Street, New York, NY 10014.

MAKEOVER MADNESS

_____
ADJECTIVE

_____
PERSON IN ROOM (FEMALE)

_____
PERSON IN ROOM (FEMALE)

_____
ADJECTIVE

_____
EXCLAMATION

_____
NOUN

_____
PART OF THE BODY

_____
PART OF THE BODY

_____
ADJECTIVE

_____
PLURAL NOUN

_____
NOUN

_____
COLOR

_____
NOUN

_____
PLURAL NOUN

_____
ADJECTIVE

_____
VERB

_____
ADVERB

_____
PLURAL NOUN

_____
NOUN

_____
PART OF THE BODY (PLURAL)

Now you've created your own hilarious MAD LIBS® game!

MAD LIBS® is fun to play with friends, but you can also play it by yourself! To begin with, DO NOT look at the story on the page below. Fill in the blanks on this page with the words called for. Then, using the words you have selected, fill in the blank spaces in the story.

MAD LIBS®

MAKEOVER MADNESS

A/An _____ scene to be played by _____ and
         ADJECTIVE   PERSON IN ROOM (FEMALE)

_____.
PERSON IN ROOM (FEMALE)

GIRL 1: I'm going to give you a/an _____ makeover.
                                        ADJECTIVE

GIRL 2: _____! Will I look like a new _____?
              EXCLAMATION   NOUN

GIRL 1: Yes, from head to _____. First, we'll brush your
                                PART OF THE BODY

_____ to make it sleek and _____.
   PART OF THE BODY   ADJECTIVE

GIRL 2: What about my _____? My friends say my eyes are my best
                            PLURAL NOUN

_____.
   NOUN

GIRL 1: They are. Applying _____ eye _____ will
                                   COLOR   NOUN

definitely bring out the color of your _____. And changing your
                                             PLURAL NOUN

_____ clothes will also help.
   ADJECTIVE

GIRL 2: You don't like the way I _____?
                                        VERB

GIRL 1: You should try and dress more _____. Those
                                              ADVERB

_____ you've been wearing are so last year. Trust me, when we're
   PLURAL NOUN

finished, you'll be the talk of the _____.
                                          NOUN

GIRL 2: I've got my _____ crossed!
                          PART OF THE BODY (PLURAL)

From SLEEPOVER PARTY MAD LIBS® • Copyright © 2008 by Price Stern Sloan,
an imprint of Penguin Group (USA) LLC, 345 Hudson Street, New York, NY 10014.

MAD LIBS® is fun to play with friends, but you can also play it by yourself! To begin with, DO NOT look at the story on the page below. Fill in the blanks on this page with the words called for. Then, using the words you have selected, fill in the blank spaces in the story.

Now you've created your own hilarious MAD LIBS® game!

HOW TO SING KARAOKE

ADJECTIVE _____

A PLACE _____

ADVERB _____

NOUN _____

ADJECTIVE _____

ADJECTIVE _____

ADJECTIVE _____

ADJECTIVE _____

ADJECTIVE _____

NOUN _____

ADVERB _____

PLURAL NOUN _____

NOUN _____

MAD LIBS®

HOW TO SING KARAOKE

Jade

Karaoke is a/an _domesticated_ form of entertainment that first became
                  ADJECTIVE

popular in (the) ~~the~~ _White house_ and _Slutty_ caught on all over
                   A PLACE   **ADVERB**

the _deer antlers_ In karaoke, you sing along to a/an _Massive_ song
      NOUN   **ADJECTIVE**

using a/an _Cocky_ microphone. You don't have to be a particularly
           ADJECTIVE

good singer to sing karaoke—you can even be a/an _dead_ singer.
                                                 ADJECTIVE

The most important thing is to have a/an _hairless_ time. Karaoke is
                                         ADJECTIVE

especially _naked_ at a sleepover party. You don't even need a/an
           ADJECTIVE

dragon machine! You can just turn up the radio and sing
NOUN

Sarcastically. Just be sure to give other _hairy legs_ a turn—you don't
ADVERB   **PLURAL NOUN**

want to be a/an _nipple_ hog!
                NOUN

MAD LIBS® is fun to play with friends, but you can also play it by yourself! To begin with, DO NOT look at the story on the page below. Fill in the blanks on this page with the words called for. Then, using the words you have selected, fill in the blank spaces in the story.

Now you've created your own hilarious MAD LIBS® game!

SLEEPOVER, SCHMEEPOVER

_____ ADJECTIVE

_____ PLURAL NOUN

_____ NUMBER

_____ NOUN

_____ NUMBER

_____ NOUN

_____ NOUN

_____ PLURAL NOUN

_____ NOUN

_____ PLURAL NOUN

_____ PLURAL NOUN

_____ NOUN

_____ PLURAL NOUN

_____ ADJECTIVE

_____ NOUN

MAD LIBS

SLEEPOVER, SCHMEEPOVER

The _____ thing about sleepover parties is that, even though you're
        ADJECTIVE

supposed to "sleep over," chances are you and your _____ will catch
                                                      PLURAL NOUN

fewer than _____ winks! It's always the same—you promise your mom
              NUMBER

and _____ that you'll go to bed before _____ o'clock, but
        NOUN   NUMBER

instead you stay up until the crack of _____. The next thing you
                                            NOUN

know, you're waking up to the smell of fried _____ and scrambled
                                                  NOUN

_____ emanating from the _____. After breakfast, you
   PLURAL NOUN   NOUN

change out of your _____, pack your _____, and stumble into
                      PLURAL NOUN   PLURAL NOUN

your parents' _____ when they come to pick you up. If you're like
                  NOUN

most _____ your age, you'll be so tired, you'll want to take a/an
        PLURAL NOUN

_____ nap the minute you get home. Which gets a/an
      ADJECTIVE

_____ thinking—maybe they should call them awake-overs instead!
   NOUN

MAD LIBS®

GRAND SLAM
MAD LIBS

by Roger Price & Leonard Stern

PSS!

PRICE STERN SLOAN

An Imprint of Penguin Group (USA) LLC

INSTRUCTIONS

MAD LIBS® is a game for people who don't like games!
It can be played by one, two, three, four, or forty.

• RIDICULOUSLY SIMPLE DIRECTIONS

In this tablet you will find stories containing blank spaces where words are left out. One player, the READER, selects one of these stories. The READER does not tell anyone what the story is about. Instead, he/she asks the other players, the WRITERS, to give him/her words. These words are used to fill in the blank spaces in the story.

• TO PLAY

The READER asks each WRITER in turn to call out a word—an adjective or a noun or whatever the space calls for—and uses them to fill in the blank spaces in the story. The result is a MAD LIBS® game.

When the READER then reads the completed MAD LIBS® game to the other players, they will discover that they have written a story that is fantastic, screamingly funny, shocking, silly, crazy, or just plain dumb—depending upon which words each WRITER called out.

• EXAMPLE (*Before* and *After*)

"_____!" he said _____
        EXCLAMATION   ADVERB

as he jumped into his convertible _____ and
                                          NOUN

drove off with his _____ wife.
                          ADJECTIVE

" *Ouch* !" he said *stupidly*
        EXCLAMATION   ADVERB

as he jumped into his convertible *cat* and
                                          NOUN

drove off with his *brave* wife.
                          ADJECTIVE

QUICK REVIEW

In case you have forgotten what adjectives, adverbs, nouns, and verbs are, here is a quick review:

An ADJECTIVE describes something or somebody. *Lumpy, soft, ugly, messy,* and *short* are adjectives.

An ADVERB tells how something is done. It modifies a verb and usually ends in "ly." *Modestly, stupidly, greedily,* and *carefully* are adverbs.

A NOUN is the name of a person, place, or thing. *Sidewalk, umbrella, bridle, bathtub,* and *nose* are nouns.

A VERB is an action word. *Run, pitch, jump,* and *swim* are verbs. Put the verbs in past tense if the directions say PAST TENSE. *Ran, pitched, jumped,* and *swam* are verbs in the past tense.

When we ask for A PLACE, we mean any sort of place: a country or city *(Spain, Cleveland)* or a room *(bathroom, kitchen).*

An EXCLAMATION or SILLY WORD is any sort of funny sound, gasp, grunt, or outcry, like *Wow!, Ouch!, Whomp!, Ick!,* and *Gadzooks!*

When we ask for specific words, like a NUMBER, a COLOR, an ANIMAL, or a PART OF THE BODY, we mean a word that is one of those things, like *seven, blue, horse,* or *head.*

When we ask for a PLURAL, it means more than one. For example, *cat* pluralized is *cats.*

THE FRIENDLY GAME
OF BASEBALL

_____ ADJECTIVE

_____ ADJECTIVE

_____ ADJECTIVE

_____ NOUN

_____ NUMBER

_____ NUMBER

_____ NOUN

_____ A PLACE

_____ NOUN

_____ NOUN

_____ ADVERB

_____ OCCUPATION

_____ VERB

_____ PLURAL NOUN

_____ PLURAL NOUN

_____ NOUN

_____ ADJECTIVE

_____ A PLACE

MAD LIBS® is fun to play with friends, but you can also play it by yourself! To begin with, DO NOT look at the story on the page below. Fill in the blanks on this page with the words called for. Then, using the words you have selected, fill in the blank spaces in the story.

Now you've created your own hilarious MAD LIBS® game!

MAD LIBS®

THE FRIENDLY GAME OF BASEBALL

Are you a/an _____ athlete looking for something
                   ADJECTIVE

_____ to do after school? Why not learn how to play the
   ADJECTIVE

_____ game of baseball? Baseball is played on a field shaped like
   ADJECTIVE

a/an _____. There are _____ teams in a league, and
       NOUN   NUMBER

each team is limited to _____ players. The teams take turns going
                              NUMBER

to bat at the _____ and playing defense in (the) _____.
                   NOUN   A PLACE

The batting team sends players up to home-_____ one at a time.
                                                    NOUN

Each player tries to hit the _____ as _____ as he can
                                   NOUN   ADVERB

and then run to first base without being tagged out by the _____.
                                                                OCCUPATION

If the player can _____ around all the bases, he scores! When you
                       VERB

score in baseball, you score _____, and the team with the most
                                 PLURAL NOUN

_____ wins the _____. Baseball is simple, it's exciting,
   PLURAL NOUN   NOUN

and it's _____. No wonder it's (the) _____'s favorite
             ADJECTIVE   A PLACE

pastime!

SPRING TRAINING

_____ A PLACE

_____ ADJECTIVE

_____ ADJECTIVE

_____ ADJECTIVE

_____ A PLACE

_____ PLURAL NOUN

_____ A PLACE

_____ PLURAL NOUN

_____ NOUN

_____ PLURAL NOUN

_____ A PLACE

_____ PLURAL NOUN

_____ ADJECTIVE

_____ PERSON IN ROOM

_____ NUMBER

_____ PLURAL NOUN

_____ ADJECTIVE

_____ NOUN

_____ PLURAL NOUN

_____ ADVERB

_____ NOUN

MAD LIBS®

SPRING TRAINING

My trip to (the) _____ for baseball spring training was
A PLACE

_____! I went with my buddy, who is a/an
ADJECTIVE

_____ fan—just like me. On the first day, we
ADJECTIVE

watched a/an _____ exhibition game between (the)
ADJECTIVE

_____ _____ and (the) _____
A PLACE   PLURAL NOUN   A PLACE

_____. Throughout the entire _____
PLURAL NOUN   NOUN

we were on the edge of our _____! The next day, we
PLURAL NOUN

watched (the) _____ _____ hold batting and
A PLACE   PLURAL NOUN

fielding practice. We quickly learned what a/an _____
ADJECTIVE

athlete _____ is. He hit _____ home
PERSON IN ROOM   NUMBER

_____! Not only is he a power hitter, he is also a/an
PLURAL NOUN

_____ defensive first _____. After practice, I asked
ADJECTIVE   NOUN

him to autograph one of the _____ I had with me, which he
PLURAL NOUN

did _____. It's now on display in my room, right next to my
ADVERB

_____ collection!
NOUN

From GRAND SLAM MAD LIBS® • Copyright © 2009 by Price Stern Sloan,
an imprint of Penguin Group (USA) LLC, 345 Hudson Street, New York, NY 10014.

RECORD BREAKERS

PLURAL NOUN _____

ADJECTIVE _____

NOUN _____

ADJECTIVE _____

ADJECTIVE _____

PERSON IN ROOM _____

ADJECTIVE _____

PLURAL NOUN _____

PERSON IN ROOM _____

ADJECTIVE _____

VERB ENDING IN "ING" _____

PERSON IN ROOM _____

NOUN _____

ADJECTIVE _____

NOUN _____

OCCUPATION _____

ADVERB _____

NOUN _____

ADJECTIVE _____

PART OF THE BODY _____

MAD LIBS® is fun to play with friends, but you can also play it by yourself! To begin with, DO NOT look at the story on the page below. Fill in the blanks on this page with the words called for. Then, using the words you have selected, fill in the blank spaces in the story.

Now you've created your own hilarious MAD LIBS® game!

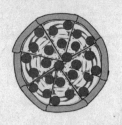

MAD LIBS®

RECORD BREAKERS

To celebrate our little league team's many _____ this season, our
PLURAL NOUN

coach took us to a/an _____ restaurant for a pizza party. At the
ADJECTIVE

_____, he gave out _____ awards to our team's most
NOUN **ADJECTIVE**

_____ players. _____ got the " _____
ADJECTIVE **PERSON IN ROOM** **ADJECTIVE**

Slugger" award for hitting the most home _____.
PLURAL NOUN

_____ won the " _____ Eye" award for having the
PERSON IN ROOM **ADJECTIVE**

best _____ average. _____ set a new record for
VERB ENDING IN "ING" **PERSON IN ROOM**

_____ stealing, and was given a/an _____ trophy.
NOUN **ADJECTIVE**

I wasn't sure if Coach had a/an _____ for me. I knew I wasn't
NOUN

the best hitter or the best _____—though I worked very
OCCUPATION

_____ all season. But, to my surprise, Coach gave me a small silver
ADVERB

_____ for being a/an _____ team player. I'm so proud,
NOUN **ADJECTIVE**

I can't wipe the smile off my _____!
PART OF THE BODY

RIGHT THROUGH HIS LEGS

_____ NOUN

_____ COLOR

_____ PLURAL NOUN

_____ A PLACE

_____ PLURAL NOUN

_____ CELEBRITY

_____ NOUN

_____ NOUN

_____ CELEBRITY

_____ ADJECTIVE

_____ NOUN

_____ ADJECTIVE

_____ PLURAL NOUN

_____ EXCLAMATION

_____ NOUN

_____ ADJECTIVE

_____ ADJECTIVE

_____ PLURAL NOUN

MAD LIBS®

RIGHT THROUGH HIS LEGS

It was game six of the _____ Series, 1986. The Boston
                           NOUN

_____ _____ were tied with (the)
     COLOR   PLURAL NOUN

_____ _____ in the bottom of the
   A PLACE   PLURAL NOUN

tenth inning when _____ stepped up to the plate. There
                        CELEBRITY

were two outs and a/an _____ on third. All Boston needed
                              NOUN

was one more _____ to bring home a victory.
                    NOUN

_____, a/an _____ sinker-ball pitcher,
     CELEBRITY   ADJECTIVE

threw a terrific _____. Getting the batter out should
                       NOUN

have been as _____ as 1-2-3, but the ball went right
                 ADJECTIVE

through the first baseman's _____. Cries of "Oh no!" and
                                 PLURAL NOUN

"_____!" were heard throughout the stands. The player on
   EXCLAMATION

third raced home and scored the winning _____. To this
                                              NOUN

day, _____ baseball fans still talk about that game and the
        ADJECTIVE

_____ loss for the Red _____.
   ADJECTIVE   PLURAL NOUN

MAD LIBS® is fun to play with friends, but you can also play it by yourself! To begin with, DO NOT look at the story on the page below. Fill in the blanks on this page with the words called for. Then, using the words you have selected, fill in the blank spaces in the story.

Now you've created your own hilarious MAD LIBS® game!

PLAYIN' BY THE RULES

_____ NOUN

_____ PLURAL NOUN

_____ ADJECTIVE

_____ NOUN

_____ NOUN

_____ NOUN

_____ PLURAL NOUN

_____ PART OF THE BODY

_____ NOUN

_____ VERB (PAST TENSE)

_____ NOUN

_____ NOUN

_____ VERB ENDING IN "S"

_____ A PLACE

_____ ADJECTIVE

_____ PLURAL NOUN

_____ ADJECTIVE

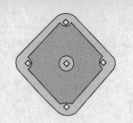
We all know the basic rules of baseball—each team tries to hit the

_____ and score as many _____ as
NOUN   PLURAL NOUN

possible. However, there are many _____ rules that
                                   ADJECTIVE

even a knowledgeable _____ might not know. For
                     NOUN

example, there's the Infield _____ Rule, which states
                             NOUN

that when a player hits a pop _____ into the infield,
                              NOUN

and there are _____ on base, the player is automatically out.
              PLURAL NOUN

The umpire throws his _____ into the air and shouts, "Infield
                      PART OF THE BODY

fly, _____ out!" Another lesser-known rule of baseball is the
     NOUN

_____ Third Strike Rule. This rule is used when the catcher
VERB (PAST TENSE)

fails to catch a/an _____ for a third strike. The umpire shouts,
                    NOUN

"_____ still in play!" The batter _____ as fast
  NOUN   VERB ENDING IN "S"

as he can, all the way to (the) _____. Now that you know these
                                A PLACE

_____ rules, you can go out to the ballpark and impress all your
ADJECTIVE

_____ with your _____ knowledge!
PLURAL NOUN   ADJECTIVE

MAD LIBS® is fun to play with friends, but you can also play it by yourself! To begin with, DO NOT look at the story on the page below. Fill in the blanks on this page with the words called for. Then, using the words you have selected, fill in the blank spaces in the story.

Now you've created your own hilarious MAD LIBS® game!

GIMME A SIGN

ADJECTIVE _____

PLURAL NOUN _____

NUMBER _____

PART OF THE BODY _____

NOUN _____

PART OF THE BODY (PLURAL) _____

ADJECTIVE _____

NOUN _____

EXCLAMATION _____

VERB (PAST TENSE) _____

PLURAL NOUN _____

PLURAL NOUN _____

NOUN _____

PART OF THE BODY _____

VERB _____

ADVERB _____

NOUN _____

NOUN _____

MAD LIBS®

GIMME A SIGN

Being a catcher isn't as _____ as it looks. Not only do I have to catch

ADJECTIVE

_____ coming at me at _____ miles an hour—I also have to
PLURAL NOUN   NUMBER

use _____ signals to tell the pitcher which _____ to throw,
PART OF THE BODY   NOUN

and those are hard to memorize! Yesterday, for example, I wanted the first pitch

to be a fastball, so I pointed two _____ to the ground. To
PART OF THE BODY (PLURAL)

my surprise, the _____ pitcher threw a/an _____-ball!
ADJECTIVE   NOUN

"_____!" I cried as the ball _____ right past me,
EXCLAMATION   VERB (PAST TENSE)

allowing all the _____ to advance. Then, when there were two
PLURAL NOUN

_____ on base and their cleanup _____ was at bat,
PLURAL NOUN   NOUN

I pointed my _____ to the ground, which means "Intentional
PART OF THE BODY

_____." But instead of _____ walking the batter,
VERB   ADVERB

the pitcher threw a curveball. The batter hit it over the fence, and we lost the

_____. As you can see, a catcher's _____ is not an
NOUN   NOUN

easy one!

From GRAND SLAM MAD LIBS® • Copyright © 2009 by Price Stern Sloan,
an imprint of Penguin Group (USA) LLC, 345 Hudson Street, New York, NY 10014.

MAD LIBS® is fun to play with friends, but you can also play it by yourself! To begin with, DO NOT look at the story on the page below. Fill in the blanks on this page with the words called for. Then, using the words you have selected, fill in the blank spaces in the story.

Now you've created your own hilarious MAD LIBS® game!

BASEBALL'S BIGGEST FAN

PLURAL NOUN _____

PLURAL NOUN _____

NOUN _____

NOUN _____

NOUN _____

CELEBRITY _____

ADJECTIVE _____

PLURAL NOUN _____

NOUN _____

ADJECTIVE _____

NOUN _____

NOUN _____

ADJECTIVE _____

ADJECTIVE _____

NOUN _____

ADVERB _____

NOUN _____

MAD LIBS®

BASEBALL'S BIGGEST FAN

I am the world's biggest fan of the game of baseball—whether it's played

by professional _____ or little league _____.
                         PLURAL NOUN   PLURAL NOUN

I watch all the games on a big-screen _____ in our
                                                    NOUN

family _____. I have a/an _____ autographed
                 NOUN   NOUN

by _____, the most _____ player who ever
           CELEBRITY   ADJECTIVE

lived. I even named my dog _____ after my favorite
                               PLURAL NOUN

_____. And when my _____ parents asked
     NOUN   ADJECTIVE

me where I'd like to go this year on vacation, I said, "Cooperstown,

of course, so I can visit the Baseball Hall of _____." This year for
                                                NOUN

my birthday I'm hoping to get a thirty-two-inch baseball _____
                                                          NOUN

made of northern white ash—just like the _____ sluggers use.
                                                ADJECTIVE

Some people go through life seeking _____ wisdom and asking
                                          ADJECTIVE

questions like "What's the meaning of _____?" and "What's the
                                        NOUN

secret to living _____?" All I want to know is, "Who's pitching and
                    ADVERB

who's on _____?"
               NOUN

SPORTY SUPERSTITIONS

NOUN _____

PLURAL NOUN _____

PERSON IN ROOM _____

NOUN _____

ADJECTIVE _____

ADJECTIVE _____

ADJECTIVE _____

PLURAL NOUN _____

PERSON IN ROOM _____

VERB _____

NUMBER _____

NOUN _____

VERB ENDING IN "ING" _____

PERSON IN ROOM _____

PART OF THE BODY _____

ARTICLE OF CLOTHING _____

NUMBER _____

PLURAL NOUN _____

NOUN _____

MAD LIBS® is fun to play with friends, but you can also play it by yourself! To begin with, DO NOT look at the story on the page below. Fill in the blanks on this page with the words called for. Then, using the words you have selected, fill in the blank spaces in the story.

Now you've created your own hilarious MAD LIBS® game!

MAD LIBS®

SPORTY SUPERSTITIONS

Our little league _____ is on a winning streak, and some of the
                    NOUN

_____ on the team are getting superstitious. _____ always
  PLURAL NOUN   PERSON IN ROOM

puts a four- _____ inside his/her baseball cap for _____.
                  NOUN   ADJECTIVE

It sounds _____, but he/she keeps catching _____
              ADJECTIVE   ADJECTIVE

high fly _____! _____ convinced that he/she needs to
            PLURAL NOUN   PERSON IN ROOM

_____ in a circle _____ times before stepping up to the
     VERB   NUMBER

_____. It works. He/She has the best _____ average on
     NOUN   VERB ENDING IN "ING"

the team. _____'s superstitions have gotten out of _____.
              PERSON IN ROOM   PART OF THE BODY

He/She has worn the same dirty _____ for _____ games
                                  ARTICLE OF CLOTHING   NUMBER

in a row! I like to win, but if it means sitting in a dugout that smells like rotten

_____, that's going beyond the call _____!
   PLURAL NOUN   NOUN

MAD LIBS® is fun to play with friends, but you can also play it by yourself! To begin with, DO NOT look at the story on the page below. Fill in the blanks on this page with the words called for. Then, using the words you have selected, fill in the blank spaces in the story.

Now you've created your own hilarious MAD LIBS® game!

TAKE ME OUT

ADJECTIVE _____

ADJECTIVE _____

VERB _____

NOUN _____

NOUN _____

TYPE OF FOOD (PLURAL) _____

PLURAL NOUN _____

ADJECTIVE _____

VERB _____

ADJECTIVE _____

VERB _____

NUMBER _____

ADJECTIVE _____

MAD LIBS®

TAKE ME OUT

Every _____ baseball game follows the _____ tradition
(ADJECTIVE)   (ADJECTIVE)

of the seventh-inning stretch. Midway through the seventh inning, you stand

up, _____, and sing this famous song:
       (VERB)

"Take me out to the ball _____.
                            (NOUN)

Take me out with the _____.
                        (NOUN)

Buy me some _____ and _____.
              (TYPE OF FOOD (PLURAL))   (PLURAL NOUN)

I don't care if I ever get _____.
                            (ADJECTIVE)

For it's root, root, _____ for the _____ team.
                      (VERB)   (ADJECTIVE)

If they don't _____ it's a shame.
               (VERB)

For it's one! Two! _____ strikes, you're out at the
                    (NUMBER)

_____ ball game!"
(ADJECTIVE)

LITTLE LEAGUE HERO

_____ ADVERB

_____ PERSON IN ROOM

_____ VERB

_____ A PLACE

_____ PLURAL NOUN

_____ ADVERB

_____ PLURAL NOUN

_____ NOUN

_____ PART OF THE BODY (PLURAL)

_____ NOUN

_____ NOUN

_____ NOUN

_____ NOUN

_____ ADJECTIVE

_____ PART OF THE BODY

_____ VERB

_____ PERSON IN ROOM

_____ PART OF THE BODY (PLURAL)

_____ ADJECTIVE

Now you've created your own hilarious MAD LIBS® game!

MAD LIBS® is fun to play with friends, but you can also play it by yourself! To begin with, DO NOT look at the story on the page below. Fill in the blanks on this page with the words called for. Then, using the words you have selected, fill in the blank spaces in the story.

MAD LIBS®

LITTLE LEAGUE HERO

Even though I practiced _____ all season long and never missed

ADVERB

any practices, Coach _____ didn't think I was ready to

PERSON IN ROOM

_____ in a real game. I finally got my shot. (The)

VERB

_____ _____ were beating us

A PLACE   PLURAL NOUN

_____, and our best player was injured. So in the

ADVERB

ninth inning, with two outs and the _____ loaded, the coach's

PLURAL NOUN

eyes searched the bench for a pinch _____. His

NOUN

_____ fell on me. He gave me the nod. I reached for

PART OF THE BODY (PLURAL)

my _____, raced to the plate, and gave the pitcher my most

NOUN

_____ stare. The pitcher threw a fast-_____.

ADJECTIVE   NOUN

I swung and hit it out of the _____ for a grand-slam home

NOUN

_____. The crowd went _____! As I ran the bases, my

NOUN   ADJECTIVE

teammates patted me on the _____ and shouted, "Way to

PART OF THE BODY

_____, _____!" Then they carried me off the

VERB   PERSON IN ROOM

field on their _____. It was the most _____

PART OF THE BODY (PLURAL)   ADJECTIVE

moment of my life!

From GRAND SLAM MAD LIBS® • Copyright © 2009 by Price Stern Sloan,
an imprint of Penguin Group (USA) LLC, 345 Hudson Street, New York, NY 10014.

THE CURSE OF
THE BILLY GOAT

_____ ANIMAL (PLURAL)

_____ VERB ENDING IN "ING"

_____ ADJECTIVE

_____ PERSON IN ROOM

_____ PLURAL NOUN

_____ ADJECTIVE

_____ ADJECTIVE

_____ PLURAL NOUN

_____ NOUN

_____ ADJECTIVE

_____ ADJECTIVE

_____ ADVERB

_____ NOUN

_____ ADJECTIVE

_____ ADJECTIVE

_____ ADVERB

_____ NOUN

MAD LIBS®

THE CURSE OF THE BILLY GOAT

The Chicago _____ are famous for their bad luck
               ANIMAL (PLURAL)

and long _____ streaks. Many people call it a/an
          VERB ENDING IN "ING"

_____ curse. As the story goes, _____,
   ADJECTIVE   PERSON IN ROOM

an immigrant from Transylvania, had two tickets to the 1945

World Series against the Detroit _____. Having no
                          PLURAL NOUN

place to leave his _____ pet goat, Dracula, he brought
             ADJECTIVE

it to the ballpark. Unfortunately, before the _____
                             ADJECTIVE

game was over, it started to rain cats and _____.
                          PLURAL NOUN

The goat, soaked to the _____, began to smell so
                   NOUN

_____ that the owner of the _____ baseball
  ADJECTIVE   ADJECTIVE

team _____ ordered the goat out of the stadium.
       ADVERB

The owner of the goat was madder than a/an _____
                             NOUN

and said he was putting a/an _____ curse on the
                   ADJECTIVE

_____ team. To this day, that team still struggles
 ADJECTIVE

_____ in postseason play. They haven't won
   ADVERB

a/an _____ Series since 1908!
     NOUN

From GRAND SLAM MAD LIBS® • Copyright © 2009 by Price Stern Sloan,
an imprint of Penguin Group (USA) LLC, 345 Hudson Street, New York, NY 10014.

BASEBALL CARDS

_____ PLURAL NOUN

_____ ADJECTIVE

_____ NOUN

_____ PLURAL NOUN

_____ PERSON IN ROOM

_____ CELEBRITY

_____ CELEBRITY

_____ EXCLAMATION

_____ ADJECTIVE

_____ PLURAL NOUN

_____ ADJECTIVE

_____ ADVERB

_____ NUMBER

_____ PLURAL NOUN

_____ ADJECTIVE

_____ VERB ENDING IN "ING"

_____ CELEBRITY

_____ NOUN

_____ PLURAL NOUN

MAD LIBS®

BASEBALL CARDS

I've been collecting baseball _____ for years. I started my

PLURAL NOUN

collection by buying a/an _____ pack of cards at the local

ADJECTIVE

_____ store. I kept the cards I liked and traded the ones

NOUN

I didn't for new _____. I made my first trade at my friend

PLURAL NOUN

_____'s house. I gave him my 2005 _____ in

PERSON IN ROOM   CELEBRITY

exchange for his 1999 _____. "_____!"

CELEBRITY   EXCLAMATION

I thought, "What a/an _____ trade!" Every weekend I would

ADJECTIVE

go to swap _____ and trade with _____

PLURAL NOUN   ADJECTIVE

collectors. My collection grew _____. I now have

ADVERB

over _____ cards! I put the valuable ones in plastic

NUMBER

_____ to keep them in _____ condition and

PLURAL NOUN   ADJECTIVE

preserve their _____ value. My favorite card, however, is

VERB ENDING IN "ING"

my 2002 _____. My dad says to guard it with my

CELEBRITY

_____—it's going to be worth hundreds of _____

NOUN   PLURAL NOUN

someday!

From GRAND SLAM MAD LIBS® • Copyright © 2009 by Price Stern Sloan,
an imprint of Penguin Group (USA) LLC, 345 Hudson Street, New York, NY 10014.

RIVALRY

PLURAL NOUN _____

NOUN _____

NUMBER _____

ADVERB _____

ADJECTIVE _____

PERSON IN ROOM (MALE) _____

ADJECTIVE _____

PLURAL NOUN _____

ADJECTIVE _____

PERSON IN ROOM _____

ADJECTIVE _____

ADJECTIVE _____

NOUN _____

VERB ENDING IN "ING" _____

ADJECTIVE _____

PLURAL NOUN _____

Now you've created your own hilarious MAD LIBS® game!

MAD LIBS® is fun to play with friends, but you can also play it by yourself! To begin with, DO NOT look at the story on the page below. Fill in the blanks on this page with the words called for. Then, using the words you have selected, fill in the blank spaces in the story.

MAD LIBS®
RIVALRY

The _____, our biggest rivals, think they're better
          PLURAL NOUN

than everyone else just because they've won the _____
                                                      NOUN

championship _____ times. They also _____ beat us in
              NUMBER   ADVERB

every _____ game last season. The only reason they won
       ADJECTIVE

is because they had _____ on their team, the
                      PERSON IN ROOM (MALE)

best _____ pitcher in the league. But he isn't playing
      ADJECTIVE

this year, so we've got a chance to beat the _____ off
                                              PLURAL NOUN

'em. And this year we've got some really _____ players.
                                          ADJECTIVE

_____, our _____ fielder, can throw all the
 PERSON IN ROOM   ADJECTIVE

way from _____ field to first _____! Also,
          ADJECTIVE   NOUN

I've been going to the batting cages every Saturday to practice my

_____ skills, so I won't strike out so much anymore. I can't wait
 VERB ENDING IN "ING"

for the _____ game against our rivals this Saturday. We'll give 'em a
         ADJECTIVE

run for their _____!
               PLURAL NOUN

COACH'S PEP TALK

PLURAL NOUN _____

NUMBER _____

ADJECTIVE _____

NOUN _____

ADJECTIVE _____

NOUN _____

EXCLAMATION _____

PART OF THE BODY _____

ADJECTIVE _____

NOUN _____

ADVERB _____

PART OF THE BODY (PLURAL) _____

NOUN _____

NOUN _____

MAD LIBS® is fun to play with friends, but you can also play it by yourself! To begin with, DO NOT look at the story on the page below. Fill in the blanks on this page with the words called for. Then, using the words you have selected, fill in the blank spaces in the story.

Now you've created your own hilarious MAD LIBS® game!

MAD LIBS®

COACH'S PEP TALK

All right, _____! Listen up! It's the bottom of the ninth, and
$\quad$ PLURAL NOUN

we're down by _____ runs. Okay, we know our opponents are a
$\quad$ NUMBER

very _____ team and they're on a winning _____
$\quad$ ADJECTIVE $\qquad$ NOUN

right now, but we can beat them. Some might say it would take a/an

_____ miracle for us to score a single _____. To that
ADJECTIVE $\qquad$ NOUN

I say: _____! We all put our pants on one _____
$\quad$ EXCLAMATION $\qquad$ PART OF THE BODY

at a time. It ain't over till the _____ lady sings! We can still win this
$\quad$ ADJECTIVE

_____ provided you think _____ and play your
NOUN $\qquad$ ADVERB

_____ out! Remember, you can do anything you put
PART OF THE BODY (PLURAL)

your _____ to. Now let's get out there and give it our best
$\quad$ NOUN

_____!
NOUN

BALLPARK CUISINE

ADJECTIVE
_____

TYPE OF LIQUID
_____

NOUN
_____

PLURAL NOUN
_____

PLURAL NOUN
_____

PLURAL NOUN
_____

PLURAL NOUN
_____

NOUN
_____

ADJECTIVE
_____

VERB
_____

NOUN
_____

PLURAL NOUN
_____

ADJECTIVE
_____

ADJECTIVE
_____

ADJECTIVE
_____

PLURAL NOUN
_____

ADJECTIVE
_____

ADJECTIVE
_____

MAD LIBS® is fun to play with friends, but you can also play it by yourself! To begin with, DO NOT look at the story on the page below. Fill in the blanks on this page with the words called for. Then, using the words you have selected, fill in the blank spaces in the story.

Now you've created your own hilarious MAD LIBS® game!

MAD LIBS®

BALLPARK CUISINE

Ah, there's nothing better than sitting in the _____
                                                    ADJECTIVE

bleachers with a cold cup of _____ and a hot ballpark
                                TYPE OF LIQUID

_____ topped with mustard, sauerkraut, and lots of
      NOUN

_____. Today, the food _____ at many
   PLURAL NOUN   PLURAL NOUN

ballparks are like five-star _____, serving everything
                               PLURAL NOUN

from soup to _____. But to the true baseball
                 PLURAL NOUN

_____, the best stuff is sold by the _____
      NOUN   ADJECTIVE

vendors, who _____ around the aisles shouting, "Get your ice-
                 VERB

cold _____! Get your roasted _____!" But
        NOUN   PLURAL NOUN

_____ dogs and cold _____ soda remain the favorite
   ADJECTIVE   ADJECTIVE

_____ food of baseball _____. Some might argue
   ADJECTIVE   PLURAL NOUN

the best part of going to a/an _____ game is the delicious,
                                  ADJECTIVE

_____ cuisine!
   ADJECTIVE

MAD LIBS' is fun to play with friends, but you can also play it by yourself! To begin with, DO NOT look at the story on the page below. Fill in the blanks on this page with the words called for. Then, using the words you have selected, fill in the blank spaces in the story.

Now you've created your own hilarious MAD LIBS' game!

SLIDERS, SINKERS, AND CURVEBALLS

_____ ADJECTIVE

_____ PLURAL NOUN

_____ NOUN

_____ PART OF THE BODY

_____ NOUN

_____ NOUN

_____ NOUN

_____ NOUN

_____ NOUN

_____ NOUN

_____ PLURAL NOUN

_____ PLURAL NOUN

_____ PART OF THE BODY

_____ NOUN

_____ NOUN

_____ NOUN

MAD LIBS®

SLIDERS, SINKERS, AND CURVEBALLS

A/An _____ pitcher today can throw a variety of
 ADJECTIVE

_____, each of which has a slightly different velocity
 PLURAL NOUN

and _____, determined by the way he holds the ball in his
 NOUN

_____. The fast-_____ is the most common
 PART OF THE BODY   NOUN

_____ in baseball and can come toward a batter faster than a speeding
 NOUN

_____, often registering ninety-five miles per _____ on the
 NOUN   NOUN

radar _____. If a pitcher alternates a fast-_____ with an
       NOUN   NOUN

off-speed pitch one called a curve or a breaking _____, he can
                                                  NOUN

tie a batter up in _____. And, if his bag of _____
                    PLURAL NOUN   PLURAL NOUN

includes a split _____ fastball and a knuckle-
                  PART OF THE BODY

_____, he is bound to be a twenty _____
 NOUN   NOUN

winner and will probably end up in the Baseball Hall of _____!
                                                         NOUN

THREE CHEERS
FOR THE UNDERDOG

_____ CELEBRITY

_____ A PLACE

_____ ADJECTIVE

_____ PART OF THE BODY

_____ VERB

_____ PERSON IN ROOM

_____ ADJECTIVE

_____ VERB

_____ NOUN

_____ ADJECTIVE

_____ PLURAL NOUN

_____ ADJECTIVE

_____ ADJECTIVE

_____ PERSON IN ROOM

_____ A PLACE

_____ PLURAL NOUN

_____ PLURAL NOUN

_____ PART OF THE BODY

MAD LIBS®

THREE CHEERS FOR THE UNDERDOG

Few people gave _____ High School any chance of advancing
                    CELEBRITY

to (the) _____ championships because of all the obstacles they
            A PLACE

faced throughout the _____ season. Their best hitter broke his
                          ADJECTIVE

_____ during the first week. Their star catcher quit the team
PART OF THE BODY

in order to _____ in the school's stage production of *Romeo*
                VERB

and _____. On top of that, a/an _____ flood
        PERSON IN ROOM   ADJECTIVE

ruined the school's practice field, forcing the team to _____ inside the
                                                          VERB

_____ for three weeks! But with _____ work and determination,
  NOUN   ADJECTIVE

these young _____ found a way to win the _____ regional
              PLURAL NOUN   ADJECTIVE

playoffs, and bring home a/an _____ trophy. How does Coach
                                  ADJECTIVE

_____ think they'll do in the state championship game against (the)
PERSON IN ROOM

_____ _____ next week? "Oh we'll give them a run for
    A PLACE   PLURAL NOUN

their _____, that's for sure. This team has a lot of _____!"
        PLURAL NOUN   PART OF THE BODY

MAD LIBS® is fun to play with friends, but you can also play it by yourself! To begin with, DO NOT look at the story on the page below. Fill in the blanks on this page with the words called for. Then, using the words you have selected, fill in the blank spaces in the story.

Now you've created your own hilarious MAD LIBS® game!

CURSE OF THE BAMBINO

_____ COLOR

_____ PLURAL NOUN

_____ LAST NAME

_____ PLURAL NOUN

_____ ADVERB

_____ PLURAL NOUN

_____ ADVERB

_____ NOUN

_____ PART OF THE BODY

_____ ADVERB

_____ VERB ENDING IN "ING"

_____ NOUN

_____ PLURAL NOUN

_____ PLURAL NOUN

_____ PERSON IN ROOM

_____ ADJECTIVE

MAD LIBS®

CURSE OF THE BAMBINO

This curse began after the owner of the Boston _____
<u>COLOR</u>

_____ traded Babe _____, sometimes
<u>PLURAL NOUN</u>   <u>LAST NAME</u>

called the Bambino, to the New York _____ at the
<u>PLURAL NOUN</u>

end of the 1919 season. Before the trade, the team was playing

_____, winning its first ever World _____
<u>ADVERB</u>   <u>PLURAL NOUN</u>

and dominating the game. But after the trade, things went

_____ wrong. They failed to win another
<u>ADVERB</u>

_____ for the next eighty-six years and endured
<u>NOUN</u>

many _____-breaking losses. New York, to whom the Bambino
<u>PART OF THE BODY</u>

was _____ traded, went on a decades-long _____
<u>ADVERB</u>   <u>VERB ENDING IN "ING"</u>

streak and dominated the American _____, winning
<u>NOUN</u>

more _____ than any other team. The Babe went
<u>PLURAL NOUN</u>

down in history as one of the greatest _____
<u>PLURAL NOUN</u>

of all time. They say that Boston spent the money from the sale

of the Bambino to pay for a theatrical production titled, *No, No,*

_____! I hope it was a/an _____ show!
<u>PERSON IN ROOM</u>   <u>ADJECTIVE</u>

From GRAND SLAM MAD LIBS® • Copyright © 2009 by Price Stern Sloan,
an imprint of Penguin Group (USA) LLC, 345 Hudson Street, New York, NY 10014.

GOING, GOING, GONE!

_____ ADJECTIVE

_____ ADJECTIVE

_____ NOUN

_____ PERSON IN ROOM

_____ NOUN

_____ PERSON IN ROOM

_____ ADJECTIVE

_____ VERB ENDING IN "ING"

_____ NOUN

_____ ADJECTIVE

_____ PART OF THE BODY

_____ NOUN

_____ PLURAL NOUN

_____ ARTICLE OF CLOTHING

_____ NOUN

_____ NOUN

_____ ADJECTIVE

_____ EXCLAMATION

_____ PLURAL NOUN

MAD LIBS® is fun to play with friends, but you can also play it by yourself! To begin with, DO NOT look at the story on the page below. Fill in the blanks on this page with the words called for. Then, using the words you have selected, fill in the blank spaces in the story.

Now you've created your own hilarious MAD LIBS® game!

MAD LIBS®

GOING, GOING, GONE!

A/An _____ sports commentary to be read aloud:
　　　　　　ADJECTIVE

Announcer #1: Well it's a/an _____ day for baseball here at
　　　　　　　　　　　　　　　　ADJECTIVE

_____ Park, and _____ is about to throw out
　　NOUN　　　　　　　　　　　PERSON IN ROOM

the first _____.
　　　　　　NOUN

Announcer #2: He's facing _____, who is a/an
　　　　　　　　　　　　　　　PERSON IN ROOM

_____ hitter with a .325 _____ average.
　ADJECTIVE　　　　　　　　　　VERB ENDING IN "ING"

Announcer #1: And here's the pitch . . . It's a/an _____-
　　　　　　　　　　　　　　　　　　　　　　　　NOUN

ball for strike one. The hitter doesn't look too _____ about it.
　　　　　　　　　　　　　　　　　　　　　　　ADJECTIVE

He is shaking his _____ and stepping outside the batter's
　　　　　　　　　PART OF THE BODY

_____ to collect his _____.
　NOUN　　　　　　　　　　　PLURAL NOUN

Announcer #2: The pitcher adjusts his _____ and
　　　　　　　　　　　　　　　　　　ARTICLE OF CLOTHING

reads the signs from his catcher. He nods, he winds up, and here's the

_____ . . .
　NOUN

Announcer #1: It's a hit! Deep to right _____! It's going . . .
　　　　　　　　　　　　　　　　　　　　　NOUN

it's going . . . it's _____! _____! A home run for
　　　　　　　　ADJECTIVE　　　　EXCLAMATION

the _____!
　　PLURAL NOUN

MAD LIBS® is fun to play with friends, but you can also play it by yourself! To begin with, DO NOT look at the story on the page below. Fill in the blanks on this page with the words called for. Then, using the words you have selected, fill in the blank spaces in the story.

Now you've created your own hilarious MAD LIBS® game!

STICKBALL

_____ ADJECTIVE

_____ ADJECTIVE

_____ VERB

_____ PLURAL NOUN

_____ NOUN

_____ PLURAL NOUN

_____ PART OF THE BODY (PLURAL)

_____ PLURAL NOUN

_____ NOUN

_____ NOUN

_____ NOUN

_____ ADJECTIVE

_____ PLURAL NOUN

_____ NOUN

MAD LIBS

STICKBALL

If you don't live near a/an _____ baseball field, you
                              ADJECTIVE

can always play stickball—a city version of baseball. You will need a/an

_____ stick, a rubber ball, and bases to _____
     ADJECTIVE   VERB

around. A lot of things in the street can be used as bases:

sewers, manhole covers, and _____. You don't need
                                  PLURAL NOUN

a pitcher in stickball—the players just toss the _____ in the
                                                      NOUN

air and hit it themselves. WARNING: You have to be careful not to hit

_____ parked along the sides of the road, and if you hit a fly
   PLURAL NOUN

ball, keep your _____ crossed it doesn't
                   PART OF THE BODY (PLURAL)

go through any glass _____. Also, if possible, play on a/an
                          PLURAL NOUN

_____ with very little _____ traffic. As long
      NOUN   NOUN

as you observe safety precautions, stickball can be just as much

_____ as the _____ game of baseball.
      NOUN   ADJECTIVE

So get all your neighborhood _____ together and play
                                  PLURAL NOUN

_____!
      NOUN

From GRAND SLAM MAD LIBS® • Copyright © 2009 by Price Stern Sloan,
an imprint of Penguin Group (USA) LLC, 345 Hudson Street, New York, NY 10014.

MAD LIBS® is fun to play with friends, but you can also play it by yourself! To begin with, DO NOT look at the story on the page below. Fill in the blanks on this page with the words called for. Then, using the words you have selected, fill in the blank spaces in the story.

Now you've created your own hilarious MAD LIBS® game!

A LEAGUE OF THEIR OWN

NOUN _____

ADJECTIVE _____

NOUN _____

VERB _____

ADJECTIVE _____

NOUN _____

A PLACE _____

A PLACE _____

PLURAL NOUN _____

NOUN _____

NOUN _____

LAST NAME _____

NOUN _____

ADJECTIVE _____

NOUN _____

PLURAL NOUN _____

NOUN _____

MAD LIBS®

A LEAGUE OF THEIR OWN

Did you know that there used to be a professional baseball

_____ for women? It was called the All-_____
NOUN   ADJECTIVE

Girls Baseball League. When America entered _____
                                                          NOUN

War II, most of the men went off to _____. In order to keep
                                            VERB

professional baseball _____, some team owners decided
                            ADJECTIVE

to make a/an _____ for women. Some team names were (the)
                  NOUN

_____ Daisies, (the) _____ Belles, and the
     A PLACE   A PLACE

Rockford _____. These _____-breaking
              PLURAL NOUN   NOUN

women inspired a movie called A/An _____ of Their
                                          NOUN

Own, which starred Tom _____ and won two
                              LAST NAME

Golden _____ awards. The _____ players
           NOUN   ADJECTIVE

were all inducted into the Baseball _____ of Fame,
                                          NOUN

and have become an inspiration to _____ everywhere.
                                        PLURAL NOUN

It goes to show that you can accomplish anything if you set your

_____ to it!
     NOUN

HOT OFF THE PRESSES
MAD LIBS

by Roger Price & Leonard Stern

PSS!
PRICE STERN SLOAN
An Imprint of Penguin Group (USA) LLC

INSTRUCTIONS

MAD LIBS® is a game for people who don't like games!
It can be played by one, two, three, four, or forty.

● RIDICULOUSLY SIMPLE DIRECTIONS

In this tablet you will find stories containing blank spaces where words are left out. One player, the READER, selects one of these stories. The READER does not tell anyone what the story is about. Instead, he/she asks the other players, the WRITERS, to give him/her words. These words are used to fill in the blank spaces in the story.

● TO PLAY

The READER asks each WRITER in turn to call out a word—an adjective or a noun or whatever the space calls for—and uses them to fill in the blank spaces in the story. The result is a MAD LIBS® game.

When the READER then reads the completed MAD LIBS® game to the other players, they will discover that they have written a story that is fantastic, screamingly funny, shocking, silly, crazy, or just plain dumb—depending upon which words each WRITER called out.

● EXAMPLE (*Before* and *After*)

"_____!" he said _____
            EXCLAMATION   ADVERB

as he jumped into his convertible _____ and
                                           NOUN

drove off with his _____ wife.
                        ADJECTIVE

"_____*Ouch*_____!" he said _____*stupidly*_____
       EXCLAMATION   ADVERB

as he jumped into his convertible _____*cat*_____ and
                                          NOUN

drove off with his _____*brave*_____ wife.
                        ADJECTIVE

QUICK REVIEW

In case you have forgotten what adjectives, adverbs, nouns, and verbs are, here is a quick review:

An ADJECTIVE describes something or somebody. *Lumpy, soft, ugly, messy,* and *short* are adjectives.

An ADVERB tells how something is done. It modifies a verb and usually ends in "ly." *Modestly, stupidly, greedily,* and *carefully* are adverbs.

A NOUN is the name of a person, place, or thing. *Sidewalk, umbrella, bridle, bathtub,* and *nose* are nouns.

A VERB is an action word. *Run, pitch, jump,* and *swim* are verbs. Put the verbs in past tense if the directions say PAST TENSE. *Ran, pitched, jumped,* and *swam* are verbs in the past tense.

When we ask for A PLACE, we mean any sort of place: a country or city *(Spain, Cleveland)* or a room *(bathroom, kitchen).*

An EXCLAMATION or SILLY WORD is any sort of funny sound, gasp, grunt, or outcry, like *Wow!, Ouch!, Whomp!, Ick!,* and *Gadzooks!*

When we ask for specific words, like a NUMBER, a COLOR, an ANIMAL, or a PART OF THE BODY, we mean a word that is one of those things, like *seven, blue, horse,* or *head.*

When we ask for a PLURAL, it means more than one. For example, *cat* pluralized is *cats.*

MAD LIBS® is fun to play with friends, but you can also play it by yourself! To begin with, DO NOT look at the story on the page below. Fill in the blanks on this page with the words called for. Then, using the words you have selected, fill in the blank spaces in the story.

Now you've created your own hilarious MAD LIBS® game!

BEHIND THE SCENES

_____ ADJECTIVE

_____ ADJECTIVE

_____ VERB ENDING IN "ING"

_____ A PLACE

_____ ADJECTIVE

_____ PLURAL NOUN

_____ PLURAL NOUN

_____ VERB

_____ ADJECTIVE

_____ PART OF THE BODY (PLURAL)

_____ VERB

_____ PART OF THE BODY

_____ SILLY WORD

_____ ADJECTIVE

_____ PLURAL NOUN

MAD LIBS®

BEHIND THE SCENES

Putting on a newscast might look easy, but it takes a lot of _____
ADJECTIVE

work. Go behind the scenes, and you'll see dozens of _____ workers
ADJECTIVE

_____ in every direction! Reporters run back and forth between
VERB ENDING IN "ING"

the studio and locations all around (the) _____ to cover _____
A PLACE   ADJECTIVE

stories and interview _____. They are joined by videographers who
PLURAL NOUN

operate handheld _____ to capture all the action. The anchors are
PLURAL NOUN

the people who _____ behind the news desk and read the stories
VERB

during the newscast. They have to look _____ on air, so they can often
ADJECTIVE

be found getting makeup applied to their _____. The director
PART OF THE BODY (PLURAL)

tells everyone where and when to _____. It's easy to spot a director
VERB

because he wears a headset on his _____ and yells things like
PART OF THE BODY

"Camera two!" and "Cut to commercial!" and "_____!" A newscast
SILLY WORD

is live television, so if you make a/an _____ mistake, everyone
ADJECTIVE

watching at home on their _____ will know!
PLURAL NOUN

MAD LIBS® is fun to play with friends, but you can also play it by yourself! To begin with, DO NOT look at the story on the page below. Fill in the blanks on this page with the words called for. Then, using the words you have selected, fill in the blank spaces in the story.

Now you've created your own hilarious MAD LIBS® game!

TODAY'S TOP STORIES

_____ ADJECTIVE

_____ NOUN

_____ A PLACE

_____ ADJECTIVE

_____ PLURAL NOUN

_____ NOUN

_____ PERSON IN ROOM

_____ NUMBER

_____ PLURAL NOUN

_____ PERSON IN ROOM

_____ NOUN

_____ PLURAL NOUN

_____ ADJECTIVE

_____ PLURAL NOUN

_____ VERB ENDING IN "ING"

_____ PLURAL NOUN

_____ CELEBRITY (MALE)

_____ PERSON IN ROOM (FEMALE)

_____ ADJECTIVE

_____ A PLACE

MAD LIBS®

TODAY'S TOP STORIES

Good morning! Here are the _____ stories we're following today:
ADJECTIVE

- A thirty-foot-high _____ struck the coast of (the)
  NOUN

  _____ earlier today, causing _____ flooding
  A PLACE   ADJECTIVE

  and forcing residents to flee to higher _____.
                                           PLURAL NOUN

- A rare watercolor _____ by renowned fifteenth-century artist
  NOUN

  _____ Van Gogh sold at auction today for the record sum
  PERSON IN ROOM

  of _____ _____.
     NUMBER   PLURAL NOUN

- _____ turns 113 today and is declared the oldest living
  PERSON IN ROOM

  _____ by the *Book of World* _____.
  NOUN   PLURAL NOUN

- New, _____ research out of the University of _____
        ADJECTIVE   PLURAL NOUN

  concludes that thirty minutes of vigorous _____ can help
                                            VERB ENDING IN "ING"

  you lose up to ten _____ in a month.
                     PLURAL NOUN

- Hollywood heartthrob _____ has married longtime love
                       CELEBRITY (MALE)

  _____ in a lavish, _____ ceremony in (the)
  PERSON IN ROOM (FEMALE)   ADJECTIVE

  _____.
  A PLACE

MAD LIBS® is fun to play with friends, but you can also play it by yourself! To begin with, DO NOT look at the story on the page below. Fill in the blanks on this page with the words called for. Then, using the words you have selected, fill in the blank spaces in the story.

Now you've created your own hilarious MAD LIBS® game!

A MORNING PERSON

_____ ADJECTIVE

_____ NOUN

_____ A PLACE

_____ VERB ENDING IN "ING"

_____ ANIMAL (PLURAL)

_____ ADJECTIVE

_____ NOUN

_____ PERSON IN ROOM

_____ ADJECTIVE

_____ VERB ENDING IN "ING"

_____ CELEBRITY

_____ PERSON IN ROOM

_____ NOUN

_____ NUMBER

_____ PLURAL NOUN

_____ VERB

MAD LIBS®

A MORNING PERSON

Devon

Are you cheery and __Cheerful__ at the crack of dawn? Do you leap out of bed
ADJECTIVE

early in the morning, ready to greet the world with a dazzling __hooters__? As
NOUN

a journalist, can you quickly switch gears from interviewing the ruler of (the)

__China__ to quizzing an expert on the effects of global __fisting__
A PLACE   VERB ENDING IN "ING"

on the planet to judging a beauty contest for __Sloth__? Then *you*
ANIMAL (PLURAL)

could be the __fluffy__ morning show host we're looking for! The number-
ADJECTIVE

one–ranked show *Good Morning,* __Sandwhich__ is searching for a cohost
NOUN

to join the current host, __Jade__. The show combines
PERSON IN ROOM

__Sexy__, hard news stories with lighter pieces such as cooking and
ADJECTIVE

__Stabbing__ segments, interviews with A-listers like __nevin__ ♡
VERB ENDING IN "ING"   CELEBRITY

and __Jade__, and fashion tips such as one hundred stylish ways to
PERSON IN ROOM

wear a feathered __hookers__. Salary is $__69__ a year plus a
NOUN   NUMBER

generous allowance for clothing and __grandmas__. Are you qualified?
PLURAL NOUN

Then __Smack__ today for an application!
VERB

BREAKING NEWS:
ALIEN ABDUCTION

NOUN _____

ADJECTIVE _____

A PLACE _____

ADJECTIVE _____

PERSON IN ROOM (FEMALE) _____

NOUN _____

ADJECTIVE _____

NOUN _____

TYPE OF LIQUID _____

PLURAL NOUN _____

PLURAL NOUN _____

PART OF THE BODY (PLURAL) _____

VERB (PAST TENSE) _____

COLOR _____

PART OF THE BODY (PLURAL) _____

NOUN _____

NOUN _____

ADJECTIVE _____

PART OF THE BODY (PLURAL) _____

MAD LIBS® is fun to play with friends, but you can also play it by yourself! To begin, DO NOT look at the story on the page below. Fill in the blanks on this page with the words called for. Then, using the words you have selected, fill in the blank spaces in the story.

Now you've created your own hilarious MAD LIBS® game!

MAD⊙LIBS®

BREAKING NEWS: ALIEN ABDUCTION

The sighting of an unidentified flying _____ was confirmed yesterday
                                         NOUN

morning over the _____ skies of (the) _____. Later that evening,
                   ADJECTIVE   A PLACE

a/an _____ resident named _____ told police she had
      ADJECTIVE   PERSON IN ROOM (FEMALE)

been the victim of a/an _____ abduction! "_____ creatures
                          NOUN   ADJECTIVE

strapped me to a long _____ and made me drink something that
                       NOUN

looked like _____ but tasted like rotten _____," she revealed.
             TYPE OF LIQUID   PLURAL NOUN

"Then they taped _____ all over my _____, and their
                  PLURAL NOUN   PART OF THE BODY (PLURAL)

machines monitored me while I _____ nonstop for what seemed
                               VERB (PAST TENSE)

like hours!" She described the aliens as having large, _____
                                                        COLOR

_____ and moving very gracefully—almost like a winged
PART OF THE BODY (PLURAL)

_____ in flight. "Finally they placed me in a/an _____-shaped
 NOUN   NOUN

spacecraft and dropped me off in a/an _____ field," she said. "I wasn't
                                       ADJECTIVE

hurt, but I learned that I prefer my _____ planted firmly on the
                                      PART OF THE BODY (PLURAL)

ground!"

MAD LIBS® is fun to play with friends, but you can also play it by yourself! To begin with, DO NOT look at the story on the page below. Fill in the blanks on this page with the words called for. Then, using the words you have selected, fill in the blank spaces in the story.

Now you've created your own hilarious MAD LIBS® game!

ALL-ACCESS PRESS PASS

PERSON IN ROOM (FEMALE) _____

NOUN _____

NOUN _____

ADJECTIVE _____

COLOR _____

CELEBRITY (MALE) _____

PART OF THE BODY (PLURAL) _____

PERSON IN ROOM _____

ADJECTIVE _____

VERB (PAST TENSE) _____

ADJECTIVE _____

PLURAL NOUN _____

PLURAL NOUN _____

ADJECTIVE _____

PART OF THE BODY (PLURAL) _____

MAD LIBS®

ALL-ACCESS PRESS PASS

Hey there! _____ here, from WFUN-TV! Guess what? I was
PERSON IN ROOM (FEMALE)

the lucky _____ assigned to cover the annual _____
NOUN   NOUN

Awards and blog about it for you! So here are the _____ details!
ADJECTIVE

First, I hit the _____ carpet and snagged interviews with
COLOR

everyone from the delicious _____, who made me weak in the
CELEBRITY (MALE)

_____, to the current Hollywood "It" kid, _____,
PART OF THE BODY (PLURAL)   PERSON IN ROOM

who's every bit as _____ in person as in the movies! I
ADJECTIVE

_____ backstage for most of the show because that's where all the
VERB (PAST TENSE)

_____ action was. And the after parties were amazing! People were
ADJECTIVE

toasting one another with glasses of chilled _____. Finally everyone
PLURAL NOUN

jumped into their chauffeured _____ and sped home—everyone
PLURAL NOUN

except me, that is. Sadly, I had to use the only mode of transportation available to

a/an _____ reporter—my own two _____!
ADJECTIVE   PART OF THE BODY (PLURAL)

MAD LIBS® is fun to play with friends, but you can also play it by yourself! To begin with, DO NOT look at the story on the page below. Fill in the blanks on this page with the words called for. Then, using the words you have selected, fill in the blank spaces in the story.

Now you've created your own hilarious MAD LIBS® game!

SPORTS RECAP

_____ NOUN

_____ SILLY WORD

_____ PART OF THE BODY

_____ ADJECTIVE

_____ NOUN

_____ PLURAL NOUN

_____ ADJECTIVE

_____ PART OF THE BODY (PLURAL)

_____ VERB

_____ SAME VERB

_____ PLURAL NOUN

_____ PERSON IN ROOM

_____ NOUN

_____ ADJECTIVE

_____ VERB ENDING IN "ING"

_____ NOUN

_____ PART OF THE BODY

_____ NOUN

_____ ADJECTIVE

_____ ADJECTIVE

MAD LIBS®

SPORTS RECAP

Devon

It was the final game of the National <u>Donald Trump</u> -ball Championships,
NOUN

and— <u>poop</u> !—it was a/an <u>but hole</u> -biter! The hometown team,
SILLY WORD   PART OF THE BODY

the <u>hairy</u> Mudslingers, was losing by just one <u>train</u> . The
ADJECTIVE   NOUN

<u>pornstars</u> were loaded, but the team was down to its last <u>fugly</u>
PLURAL NOUN   ADJECTIVE

batter—and the final pitch. The sold-out crowd was on its <u>toes</u> ,
PART OF THE BODY (PLURAL)

screaming " <u>punch</u> , Mudslingers, <u>punch</u> !" and waving giant
VERB   SAME VERB

foam <u>wizards</u> . The pitch to star player <u>Jodie</u> was
PLURAL NOUN   PERSON IN ROOM

perfect, and—crack!—the <u>stripclub</u> was airborne. The <u>shitty</u>
NOUN   ADJECTIVE

outfielder took off <u>fisting</u> toward the fence with his <u>Chucky</u>
VERB ENDING IN "ING"   NOUN

outstretched to catch the ball—but all he could do was watch it sail over his

<u>armpit</u> and into the stands. One <u>football</u> scored, then another!
PART OF THE BODY   NOUN

The crowd went absolutely <u>bald</u> ! The Mudslingers won the game that
ADJECTIVE

day—and the hearts of their <u>smelly</u> fans forever!
ADJECTIVE

MAN ON THE STREET INTERVIEWS

_____ A PLACE

_____ ADJECTIVE

_____ PERSON IN ROOM (FEMALE)

_____ A PLACE

_____ PLURAL NOUN

_____ NOUN

_____ NOUN

_____ CELEBRITY

_____ NOUN

_____ PART OF THE BODY (PLURAL)

_____ ADJECTIVE

_____ PERSON IN ROOM

_____ A PLACE

_____ PART OF THE BODY

_____ VERB

_____ PERSON IN ROOM (MALE)

_____ NOUN

MAD LIBS®

MAN ON THE STREET INTERVIEWS

This is roving reporter Perry Winkle, and I'm here in (the) _____ to
A PLACE

ask folks today's random question: *What is the first thing you would do if you ruled*

the world? Responses ranged from intelligent to downright _____.
ADJECTIVE

Here's a sampling:

- _____ from (the) _____ said, "I'd make
  PERSON IN ROOM (FEMALE) A PLACE

  sure everyone had plenty of healthy _____ to eat and a warm,
  PLURAL NOUN

  safe _____ to live in."
  NOUN

- An up-and-coming _____ by the name of _____ said, "I
  NOUN CELEBRITY

  would give each man, woman, and _____ a job. It's important to
  NOUN

  use your mind or your _____ to work and make the world
  PART OF THE BODY (PLURAL)

  a/an _____ place."
  ADJECTIVE

- _____ from (the) _____ said, "There'd be no wars.
  PERSON IN ROOM A PLACE

  People would only be allowed to _____ wrestle one another, but
  PART OF THE BODY

  then they'd _____ and make up.
  VERB

- Local comedian _____ said, "I would require every citizen
  PERSON IN ROOM (MALE)

  to address me by my superhero name—_____-man!"
  NOUN

MAD LIBS® is fun to play with friends, but you can also play it by yourself! To begin with, DO NOT look at the story on the page below. Fill in the blanks on this page with the words called for. Then, using the words you have selected, fill in the blank spaces in the story.

Now you've created your own hilarious MAD LIBS® game!

TRAFFIC REPORT

_____ PLURAL NOUN

_____ ADJECTIVE

_____ VERB

_____ NUMBER

_____ NOUN

_____ A PLACE

_____ PLURAL NOUN

_____ ADJECTIVE

_____ PART OF THE BODY (PLURAL)

_____ NOUN

_____ CELEBRITY

_____ ADJECTIVE

_____ PLURAL NOUN

_____ NOUN

_____ PERSON IN ROOM

_____ NOUN

_____ NOUN

_____ NOUN

MAD LIBS®

TRAFFIC REPORT

Folks, I hate to be the bearer of bad _____, but it's a slow-go on today's
　　　　　　　　　　　　　　　PLURAL NOUN

_____ roadways. Everyone seems to have forgotten how to _____
ADJECTIVE　　　　　　　　　　　　　　　　　　　　　　　　　　　　VERB

behind the wheel! There's a/an _____-_____ pileup on Route
　　　　　　　　　　　　　　NUMBER　　　　　NOUN

86 that's got traffic backed up all the way to (the) _____! Police and
　　　　　　　　　　　　　　　　　　　　　　　A PLACE

emergency _____ are on the scene, but those _____
　　　　　　PLURAL NOUN　　　　　　　　　　　　　　　　　ADJECTIVE

drivers craning their _____ to see what's going on aren't
　　　　　　　　　PART OF THE BODY (PLURAL)

helping matters. A car with a flat _____ is causing a slowdown on
　　　　　　　　　　　　　　　　NOUN

_____ Highway. A/An _____ semitruck headed downtown
CELEBRITY　　　　　　　　　　ADJECTIVE

has jackknifed, spilling its load of frozen _____. And here's something
　　　　　　　　　　　　　　　　　　　　PLURAL NOUN

you don't see every day: A two-hundred-pound _____ by the
　　　　　　　　　　　　　　　　　　　　　　NOUN

name of _____ escaped from the zoo and wandered into the path
　　　PERSON IN ROOM

of an oncoming _____, which then swerved and crashed into a/an
　　　　　　NOUN

_____. Let's face it, folks—today's a day where you need patience, a
NOUN

sense of humor, or a flying _____!
　　　　　　　　　　　NOUN

MAD LIBS® is fun to play with friends, but you can also play it by yourself! To begin with, DO NOT look at the story on the page below. Fill in the blanks on this page with the words called for. Then, using the words you have selected, fill in the blank spaces in the story.

Now you've created your own hilarious MAD LIBS® game!

THAT'S CLASSIFIED INFORMATION

_____ ADJECTIVE

_____ ADJECTIVE

_____ NOUN

_____ PERSON IN ROOM

_____ ADJECTIVE

_____ PLURAL NOUN

_____ NUMBER

_____ PLURAL NOUN

_____ PLURAL NOUN

_____ NOUN

_____ NOUN

_____ ADJECTIVE

_____ PLURAL NOUN

_____ NOUN

_____ PLURAL NOUN

_____ ADJECTIVE

_____ PLURAL NOUN

MAD LIBS®

THAT'S CLASSIFIED INFORMATION

Got junk? Sell your unwanted stuff in our _____ classified section!
ADJECTIVE

Today's _____ deals include a/an:
ADJECTIVE

- Baby grand _____ previously owned by legendary pianist
  NOUN

  _____ "_____ Hands" O'Hara. Asking two thousand
  PERSON IN ROOM   ADJECTIVE

  _____ or best offer
  PLURAL NOUN

- _____-piece collection of rare _____ finely crafted from ceramic,
  NUMBER   PLURAL NOUN

  porcelain, and gold-plated _____
                              PLURAL NOUN

- Cage, feeding bowl, and hand-knitted _____ for a pet
                                        NOUN

  _____
  NOUN

- _____ minifridge, perfect for holding bottles of _____
  ADJECTIVE   PLURAL NOUN

- Used pickup_____ with one hundred thousand _____
             NOUN   PLURAL NOUN

  and _____ bumper sticker stating "Honk if you love _____!"
      ADJECTIVE   PLURAL NOUN

MAD LIBS® is fun to play with friends, but you can also play it by yourself! To begin with, DO NOT look at the story on the page below. Fill in the blanks on this page with the words called for. Then, using the words you have selected, fill in the blank spaces in the story.

Now you've created your own hilarious MAD LIBS® game!

TALK SHOW QUEEN

NUMBER _____

NOUN _____

PERSON IN ROOM (FEMALE) _____

ADJECTIVE _____

PART OF THE BODY _____

NOUN _____

PERSON IN ROOM (MALE) _____

CELEBRITY (FEMALE) _____

PART OF THE BODY _____

NUMBER _____

NOUN _____

NOUN _____

ADJECTIVE _____

ADJECTIVE _____

A PLACE _____

MAD LIBS®

TALK SHOW QUEEN

After a/an _____-year reign as daytime TV's most popular talk show
           NUMBER

_____, _____ O'Walters finally announced her
  NOUN   PERSON IN ROOM (FEMALE)

retirement. On her _____ farewell show, she recalled the moments
             ADJECTIVE

nearest and dearest to her _____:
             PART OF THE BODY

- When famed Hollywood actor and leading _____,
            NOUN

  _____, proclaimed his love for _____—then
    PERSON IN ROOM (MALE)   CELEBRITY (FEMALE)

  surprised everyone by getting down on one _____ and proposing
              PART OF THE BODY

  with a/an _____-karat diamond _____.
       NUMBER   NOUN

- When a woman and the _____ she gave up for adoption twenty
           NOUN

  years earlier were reunited.

- When each member of the _____ audience was given a fully
           ADJECTIVE

  loaded, fuel-efficient _____ convertible and an all-expenses-paid
          ADJECTIVE

  trip to (the) _____.
        A PLACE

BREAKING NEWS: BIGFOOT SPOTTED

_____ NOUN

_____ NOUN

_____ ADJECTIVE

_____ PART OF THE BODY

_____ NOUN

_____ PLURAL NOUN

_____ PLURAL NOUN

_____ PLURAL NOUN

_____ PERSON IN ROOM

_____ NOUN

_____ ANIMAL

_____ PART OF THE BODY (PLURAL)

_____ VERB ENDING IN "ING"

_____ VERB ENDING IN "ING"

_____ PART OF THE BODY

_____ PERSON IN ROOM

_____ VERB (PAST TENSE)

MAD LIBS

BREAKING NEWS: BIGFOOT SPOTTED

A/An _____ Scout troop camping in a remote location inside
         NOUN

_____ National Forest reported a/an _____ encounter
      NOUN   ADJECTIVE

with the elusive creature known as Big-_____. "It was dusk. The
                                              PART OF THE BODY

_____ had just begun to set when we finished pitching our
      NOUN

_____. We set out to gather _____ to make a fire
   PLURAL NOUN   PLURAL NOUN

so we could roast some _____ for s'mores," said troop leader
                              PLURAL NOUN

_____. "We were just about to head back to camp when we heard
   PERSON IN ROOM

a/an _____ snap loudly nearby. We figured it was a squirrel or a/an
            NOUN

_____, but then we saw a pair of _____
        ANIMAL   PART OF THE BODY (PLURAL)

watching us from the darkness." The troop leader told how they took off

_____ as fast as they could through the forest and hid inside
   VERB ENDING IN "ING"

their _____ bags all night. "I was scared out of my _____,"
        VERB ENDING IN "ING"   PART OF THE BODY

said nine-year-old _____. "I don't think I _____ more
                        PERSON IN ROOM   VERB (PAST TENSE)

than five minutes all night."

CONCERT REVIEW

ADJECTIVE

_____

COLOR

_____

ANIMAL (PLURAL)

_____

VERB ENDING IN "ING"

_____

PLURAL NOUN

_____

PERSON IN ROOM

_____

PART OF THE BODY

_____

PART OF THE BODY (PLURAL)

_____

ADJECTIVE

_____

PLURAL NOUN

_____

ADJECTIVE

_____

NOUN

_____

VERB ENDING IN "ING"

_____

ADJECTIVE

_____

PERSON IN ROOM (FEMALE)

_____

PART OF THE BODY

_____

COLOR

_____

ARTICLE OF CLOTHING

_____

NOUN

_____

PLURAL NOUN

_____

MAD LIBS° is fun to play with friends, but you can also play it by yourself! To begin with, DO NOT look at the story on the page below. Fill in the blanks on this page with the words called for. Then, using the words you have selected, fill in the blank spaces in the story.

Now you've created your own hilarious MAD LIBS° game!

MAD LIBS®
CONCERT REVIEW

The _____ _____ _____ performed
    ADJECTIVE   COLOR   ANIMAL (PLURAL)

last night and wowed the _____-room-only crowd of screaming
                      VERB ENDING IN "ING"

_____. Music Editor _____ was there and had this
  PLURAL NOUN   PERSON IN ROOM

to report:

"What a/an _____-blowing show! My _____ are
     PART OF THE BODY   PART OF THE BODY (PLURAL)

still ringing! The band performed all their _____ hits, like "Too Cool
                       ADJECTIVE

for _____" and "Best _____ Friends Forever." Between the
   PLURAL NOUN   ADJECTIVE

music and the awesome laser _____ show, the crowd was on its feet and
                NOUN

_____ to the beat the whole night. But the music and lights were
VERB ENDING IN "ING"

almost overshadowed by the many _____ costume changes by lead
                    ADJECTIVE

singer Lady _____. It was hard to decide which was
       PERSON IN ROOM (FEMALE)

more _____-dropping—the _____ leather
   PART OF THE BODY   COLOR

_____ and _____-shaped headpiece she wore or the
 ARTICLE OF CLOTHING   NOUN

simple gown fashioned completely from _____."
                  PLURAL NOUN

AND IN LOCAL NEWS

_____ ADJECTIVE

_____ NOUN

_____ PLURAL NOUN

_____ NOUN

_____ NOUN

_____ PERSON IN ROOM

_____ NOUN

_____ NOUN

_____ NOUN

_____ ADJECTIVE

_____ NOUN

_____ PLURAL NOUN

_____ PLURAL NOUN

_____ ADJECTIVE

_____ PLURAL NOUN

_____ NOUN

MAD LIBS®

AND IN LOCAL NEWS

Small-town life doesn't mean big things don't happen! Here are some of the

_____ events taking place this weekend and next in Little
ADJECTIVE

_____ Falls:
NOUN

- Stop by the Brotherhood of the _____ Lodge on Sunday for an all-
PLURAL NOUN

you-can-eat _____ breakfast to benefit the town's _____
NOUN   NOUN

rescue shelter. Mayor _____ will be flipping hotcakes and grilling
PERSON IN ROOM

_____ patties.
NOUN

- Join us for the grand opening of the town's first _____ Mart! A
NOUN

limited edition _____ will be given away to the first one hundred
NOUN

_____ shoppers.
ADJECTIVE

- Next weekend is the annual _____ festival. Vendors will be selling
NOUN

fresh-picked _____, and baked _____ will be available. Come
PLURAL NOUN   PLURAL NOUN

hungry—and leave _____!
ADJECTIVE

- Mark your calendar for the community garage sale. Unearth your unused

_____ and sell them for a few bucks. Remember—one man's
PLURAL NOUN

_____ is another man's treasure!
NOUN

WARNING: SEVERE WEATHER

_____ ADJECTIVE

_____ A PLACE

_____ ADJECTIVE

_____ PLURAL NOUN

_____ PLURAL NOUN

_____ VERB ENDING IN "ING"

_____ NOUN

_____ ADJECTIVE

_____ NOUN

_____ NOUN

_____ PART OF THE BODY

_____ NOUN

_____ VERB ENDING IN "ING"

_____ TYPE OF LIQUID

_____ VERB

_____ PART OF THE BODY (PLURAL)

_____ ADJECTIVE

MAD LIBS®

WARNING: SEVERE WEATHER

Our radar shows a line of _____ weather stretching from the midwest
                              ADJECTIVE

plains all the way to the coast of (the) _____. This weather pattern is
                                          A PLACE

producing _____ thunderstorms with heavy rains, _____
           ADJECTIVE   PLURAL NOUN

gusting up to eighty mph, and hail the size of _____! Tornado
                                                 PLURAL NOUN

warnings are in effect for most of the viewing area. A funnel cloud was spotted

_____ across an open field and destroying every _____
VERB ENDING IN "ING"   NOUN

in its path. Remember, in the event of a/an _____ tornado, head to
                                              ADJECTIVE

the basement or climb into the nearest _____ and pull a/an
                                          NOUN

_____ over you so that your _____ is protected. If
   NOUN   PART OF THE BODY

you're out driving around in your _____, be on the lookout for
                                     NOUN

flash _____ in low-lying areas. If you get caught in rushing
      VERB ENDING IN "ING"

_____, climb out of your vehicle and _____ for
TYPE OF LIQUID   VERB

your life! Stay tuned to this channel—and keep your _____
                                                       PART OF THE BODY (PLURAL)

to the sky—for _____ weather-related updates.
                 ADJECTIVE

From HOT OFF THE PRESSES MAD LIBS® • Copyright © 2012 by Price Stern Sloan,
an imprint of Penguin Group (USA) LLC, 345 Hudson Street, New York, NY 10014.

MAD LIBS® is fun to play with friends, but you can also play it by yourself! To begin with, DO NOT look at the story on the page below. Fill in the blanks on this page with the words called for. Then, using the words you have selected, fill in the blank spaces in the story.

Now you've created your own hilarious MAD LIBS® game!

HOW TO GET THE SCOOP

_____ ADJECTIVE

_____ ADJECTIVE

_____ NOUN

_____ VERB

_____ NOUN

_____ NOUN

_____ PART OF THE BODY

_____ ADJECTIVE

_____ VERB ENDING IN "ING"

_____ PLURAL NOUN

_____ PLURAL NOUN

_____ ADJECTIVE

_____ NOUN

_____ PLURAL NOUN

_____ VERB ENDING IN "ING"

_____ ADJECTIVE

MAD LIBS®

HOW TO GET THE SCOOP

Do you have a/an _____ nose for news? Here are _____
          ADJECTIVE   ADJECTIVE

tips for becoming a/an _____-winning investigative journalist:
                          NOUN

1. March up to a person's front door and _____. When they answer
                                               VERB

    the _____, stick your micro-_____ right under their
           NOUN   NOUN

    _____ and start firing questions.
        PART OF THE BODY

2. Ask as many _____ questions as possible. Getting someone
                      ADJECTIVE

    to break down and start _____ is great.
                            VERB ENDING IN "ING"

3. Seek out a person's family and _____. Offer the large
                                        PLURAL NOUN

    amounts of _____ to tell you everything they know.
                PLURAL NOUN

4. Assemble a/an _____ disguise to go undercover. An oversize
                       ADJECTIVE

    _____ to wear across your face and a fake pair of _____
        NOUN   PLURAL NOUN

    work well.

5. Practice _____ as fast as you can so, when necessary, you can
               VERB ENDING IN "ING"

    make a/an _____ getaway.
                 ADJECTIVE

SUMMER MOVIE REVIEWS

ADJECTIVE _____

NOUN _____

NOUN _____

PLURAL NOUN _____

PERSON IN ROOM (MALE) _____

ADJECTIVE _____

ADJECTIVE _____

PLURAL NOUN _____

ADJECTIVE _____

PERSON IN ROOM (MALE) _____

ANIMAL _____

SAME ANIMAL _____

ADJECTIVE _____

VERB _____

PERSON IN ROOM (FEMALE) _____

NOUN _____

ADJECTIVE _____

PLURAL NOUN _____

PERSON IN ROOM (MALE) _____

Now you've created your own hilarious MAD LIBS® game!

MAD LIBS® is fun to play with friends, but you can also play it by yourself! To begin with, DO NOT look at the story on the page below. Fill in the blanks on this page with the words called for. Then, using the words you have selected, fill in the blank spaces in the story.

MAD LIBS®

SUMMER MOVIE REVIEWS

It's summer, and you know what that means: _____ weather, icy-
ADJECTIVE

cold _____-sicles, and big blockbusters. Check out what's coming to a/an
NOUN

_____ near you this summer!
NOUN

• _____ of the Caribbean: Captain _____ and his
PLURAL NOUN   PERSON IN ROOM (MALE)

band of _____ scalawags take to the _____ seas in search of
ADJECTIVE   ADJECTIVE

buried _____.
PLURAL NOUN

• The Big _____ Ogre: A cranky ogre named _____,
ADJECTIVE   PERSON IN ROOM (MALE)

his sidekick—a/an _____ named _____—and a/an
ANIMAL   SAME ANIMAL

_____ gang of fairy-tale creatures go on a search and _____
ADJECTIVE   VERB

mission to rescue Princess _____ from a tower guarded by a fire-
PERSON IN ROOM (FEMALE)

breathing _____.
NOUN

• The Boy Wizard: A/An _____ boy discovers he possesses magical
ADJECTIVE

_____ that he must use to defeat the evil wizard, Lord
PLURAL NOUN

_____.
PERSON IN ROOM (MALE)

CELEBRITY INTERVIEW

VERB _____

NOUN _____

PERSON IN ROOM _____

PART OF THE BODY _____

ADJECTIVE _____

NOUN _____

ADJECTIVE _____

NOUN _____

ADJECTIVE _____

ADJECTIVE _____

PLURAL NOUN _____

PART OF THE BODY _____

NOUN _____

ADJECTIVE _____

NUMBER _____

MAD LIBS® is fun to play with friends, but you can also play it by yourself! To begin with, DO NOT look at the story on the page below. Fill in the blanks on this page with the words called for. Then, using the words you have selected, fill in the blank spaces in the story.

Now you've created your own hilarious MAD LIBS® game!

MAD LIBS

CELEBRITY INTERVIEW

Movie critic Daisy Meadows had the chance to _____ with
                                                    VERB

international _____ star Brad Kluney and chat about his new
                  NOUN

project, The _____ Chronicles.
               PERSON IN ROOM

Daisy: Forgive me if I'm a bit _____-tied. I'm such a/an
                                      PART OF THE BODY

_____ fan of yours! You're the handsomest _____ I've ever
   ADJECTIVE   NOUN

laid eyes on.

Brad: That's so _____ of you to say.
                       ADJECTIVE

Daisy: So, Brad, in this movie, are you a good _____ or a/an
                                                        NOUN

_____ guy?
   ADJECTIVE

Brad: I play a/an _____ guy who gets mixed up with some _____
                         ADJECTIVE   PLURAL NOUN

who may or may not be on the wrong side of the law. I spend a lot of the movie

thoughtfully scratching my _____.
                              PART OF THE BODY

Daisy: There's already buzz that this role will earn you a/an _____
                                                                     NOUN

Award nomination.

Brad: A happy, _____ audience is all I want—and
                      ADJECTIVE

my _____-dollar salary.
      NUMBER

BREAKING NEWS: LOST CITY FOUND

ADJECTIVE _____

A PLACE _____

ADJECTIVE _____

SILLY WORD _____

PLURAL NOUN _____

ADJECTIVE _____

PLURAL NOUN _____

PART OF THE BODY _____

ANIMAL _____

PART OF THE BODY _____

ANIMAL _____

CELEBRITY _____

ADJECTIVE _____

NOUN _____

PERSON IN ROOM _____

PART OF THE BODY (PLURAL) _____

MAD LIBS® is fun to play with friends, but you can also play it by yourself! To begin with, DO NOT look at the story on the page below. Fill in the blanks on this page with the words called for. Then, using the words you have selected, fill in the blank spaces in the story.

Now you've created your own hilarious MAD LIBS® game!

MAD LIBS®

BREAKING NEWS: LOST CITY FOUND

A/An _____ archeological team working in the remote jungles of (the)
ADJECTIVE

_____ have reportedly discovered the _____ ancient city of
A PLACE   ADJECTIVE

_____ buried under about ten miles of _____. The team
SILLY WORD   PLURAL NOUN

said they knew they had stumbled onto something _____ when they
ADJECTIVE

unearthed weapons, tools, and _____ handcrafted from pure gold
PLURAL NOUN

and bearing the city's symbol—a mythical creature with the _____ of
PART OF THE BODY

a/an _____ and the _____ of a/an _____. If
ANIMAL   PART OF THE BODY   ANIMAL

that weren't proof enough, Chief Archeologist Dr. _____ said they
CELEBRITY

were certain it was the ancient city when they found a tomb marked with the

name of the city's legendary, _____ ruler, Ah-Ah-Achooey-Kaboom-
ADJECTIVE

Boom, which roughly translates to "one who sneezes as explosively as a/an _____
NOUN

erupting." "It's incredible," said Junior Archeologist _____. "I never
PERSON IN ROOM

would have believed this place existed if I hadn't seen it with my own two

_____."
PART OF THE BODY (PLURAL)

DARE TO BE NEWSWORTHY

PLURAL NOUN _____

ADJECTIVE _____

PERSON IN ROOM (MALE) _____

NOUN _____

PLURAL NOUN _____

ARTICLE OF CLOTHING _____

PERSON IN ROOM (FEMALE) _____

COLOR _____

VERB (PAST TENSE) _____

PLURAL NOUN _____

PERSON IN ROOM (MALE) _____

NUMBER _____

PLURAL NOUN _____

PART OF THE BODY _____

A PLACE _____

A PLACE _____

PERSON IN ROOM (FEMALE) _____

CELEBRITY (MALE) _____

MAD LIBS® is fun to play with friends, but you can also play it by yourself! To begin with, DO NOT look at the story on the page below. Fill in the blanks on this page with the words called for. Then, using the words you have selected, fill in the blank spaces in the story.

Now you've created your own hilarious MAD LIBS® game!

MAD LIBS®

DARE TO BE NEWSWORTHY

Some people will do anything to get their fifteen minutes of _____.
                                                          PLURAL NOUN

Think you've seen it all? Check out the _____ things these people
                                        ADJECTIVE

did to make headlines:

- _____, a star _____-ball player at his school,
  PERSON IN ROOM (MALE)   NOUN

  ran a marathon wearing 5-inch stiletto _____ and a skintight,
                                          PLURAL NOUN

  floral _____.
         ARTICLE OF CLOTHING

- _____ painted herself bright _____ and
  PERSON IN ROOM (FEMALE)   COLOR

  _____ in a public fountain while people blasted her with squirt
  VERB (PAST TENSE)

  guns filled with _____.
                   PLURAL NOUN

- _____ tied _____ helium-filled
  PERSON IN ROOM (MALE)   NUMBER

  _____ around his _____ and floated from (the)
  PLURAL NOUN   PART OF THE BODY

  _____ to (the) _____.
  A PLACE   A PLACE

- _____ walked up to every fast-food drive-through window
  PERSON IN ROOM (FEMALE)

  in town and asked if she could have _____ to go.
                                      CELEBRITY (MALE)

MAD LIBS® is fun to play with friends, but you can also play it by yourself! To begin with, DO NOT look at the story on the page below. Fill in the blanks on this page with the words called for. Then, using the words you have selected, fill in the blank spaces in the story.

Now you've created your own hilarious MAD LIBS® game!

POLITICAL DEBATE

ADJECTIVE _____

COLOR _____

NOUN _____

ADJECTIVE _____

VERB ENDING IN "ING" _____

NOUN _____

PLURAL NOUN _____

ADJECTIVE _____

PLURAL NOUN _____

ADJECTIVE _____

NOUN _____

TYPE OF LIQUID _____

MAD LIBS

POLITICAL DEBATE

Welcome to another edition of *Meet the* _____ *Candidates*! Today we
                                              ADJECTIVE

have Jessica and Justin from _____ Valley High School. Both of
                                   COLOR

them are running for student council _____. Let's listen as they share
                                            NOUN

their _____ ideas for leadership.
            ADJECTIVE

Jessica: I believe that teachers should assign _____ homework every
                                                  VERB ENDING IN "ING"

night.

Justin: I will fight for the cafeteria's right to serve _____ tots every day
                                                            NOUN

at lunch and steamed _____ only once a week.
                       PLURAL NOUN

Jessica: I will make sure our library is stocked with the latest _____
                                                                        ADJECTIVE

best sellers.

Justin: I will keep our vending machines stocked with _____.
                                                          PLURAL NOUN

Jessica: A vote for me is a vote for a clean, safe, _____ school where
                                                          ADJECTIVE

each and every _____ can excel!
                   NOUN

Justin: A vote for me ensures drinking fountains are filled with clean, fresh

_____. Yum!
  TYPE OF LIQUID

LOCAL HERO BECOMES SENSATION

_____
PERSON IN ROOM (MALE)

_____
ADJECTIVE

_____
NOUN

_____
A PLACE

_____
VERB ENDING IN "ING"

_____
NOUN

_____
PLURAL NOUN

_____
VERB

_____
ADJECTIVE

_____
PART OF THE BODY

_____
NOUN

_____
ADJECTIVE

_____
NOUN

_____
PART OF THE BODY

_____
TYPE OF LIQUID

_____
NOUN

_____
PERSON IN ROOM (FEMALE)

_____
PART OF THE BODY

_____
NOUN

MAD LIBS® is fun to play with friends, but you can also play it by yourself! To begin with, DO NOT look at the story on the page below. Fill in the blanks on this page with the words called for. Then, using the words you have selected, fill in the blank spaces in the story.

Now you've created your own hilarious MAD LIBS® game!

MAD LIBS®

LOCAL HERO BECOMES SENSATION

_____ "The Truck" MacAllister didn't consider himself a
PERSON IN ROOM (MALE)

hero—except when he made a/an _____ play on the _____-
ADJECTIVE   NOUN

ball field. But residents of (the) _____ begged to differ. MacAllister
A PLACE

happened to be _____ by a bank when a masked
VERB ENDING IN "ING"

_____ came running out carrying a bag of stolen _____.
NOUN   PLURAL NOUN

MacAllister didn't stop to _____—he just sprinted after the
VERB

_____ thief and tackled him. MacAllister held the robber in a/an
ADJECTIVE

_____-lock until police arrived. He didn't know that a pedestrian
PART OF THE BODY

had caught it all on video and posted it on _____-Tube. It was a/an
NOUN

_____ hit, and MacAllister became an overnight _____!
ADJECTIVE   NOUN

Strangers wanted to shake his _____. Restaurants gave him free
PART OF THE BODY

_____. A lovely _____ named _____
TYPE OF LIQUID   NOUN   PERSON IN ROOM (FEMALE)

even proposed marriage! But he never let fame go to his _____. "I'm
PART OF THE BODY

just a simple _____ who was in the right place at the right time," he
NOUN

said.

MAD SCIENTIST
MAD LIBS

concept created by Roger Price & Leonard Stern

PSS!

PRICE STERN SLOAN

An Imprint of Penguin Group (USA) LLC

INSTRUCTIONS

MAD LIBS® is a game for people who don't like games!
It can be played by one, two, three, four, or forty.

• RIDICULOUSLY SIMPLE DIRECTIONS

In this tablet you will find stories containing blank spaces where words are left out. One player, the READER, selects one of these stories. The READER does not tell anyone what the story is about. Instead, he/she asks the other players, the WRITERS, to give him/her words. These words are used to fill in the blank spaces in the story.

• TO PLAY

The READER asks each WRITER in turn to call out a word—an adjective or a noun or whatever the space calls for—and uses them to fill in the blank spaces in the story. The result is a MAD LIBS® game.

When the READER then reads the completed MAD LIBS® game to the other players, they will discover that they have written a story that is fantastic, screamingly funny, shocking, silly, crazy, or just plain dumb—depending upon which words each WRITER called out.

• EXAMPLE (*Before* and *After*)

"_____!" he said _____
     EXCLAMATION   ADVERB

as he jumped into his convertible _____ and
                                              NOUN

drove off with his _____ wife.
                        ADJECTIVE

"_____*Ouch*_____!" he said _____*stupidly*_____
     EXCLAMATION   ADVERB

as he jumped into his convertible _____*cat*_____ and
                                              NOUN

drove off with his _____*brave*_____ wife.
                        ADJECTIVE

QUICK REVIEW

In case you have forgotten what adjectives, adverbs, nouns, and verbs are, here is a quick review:

An ADJECTIVE describes something or somebody. *Lumpy, soft, ugly, messy,* and *short* are adjectives.

An ADVERB tells how something is done. It modifies a verb and usually ends in "ly." *Modestly, stupidly, greedily,* and *carefully* are adverbs.

A NOUN is the name of a person, place, or thing. *Sidewalk, umbrella, bridle, bathtub,* and *nose* are nouns.

A VERB is an action word. *Run, pitch, jump,* and *swim* are verbs. Put the verbs in past tense if the directions say PAST TENSE. *Ran, pitched, jumped,* and *swam* are verbs in the past tense.

When we ask for A PLACE, we mean any sort of place: a country or city *(Spain, Cleveland)* or a room *(bathroom, kitchen).*

An EXCLAMATION or SILLY WORD is any sort of funny sound, gasp, grunt, or outcry, like *Wow!, Ouch!, Whomp!, Ick!,* and *Gadzooks!*

When we ask for specific words, like a NUMBER, a COLOR, an ANIMAL, or a PART OF THE BODY, we mean a word that is one of those things, like *seven, blue, horse,* or *head.*

When we ask for a PLURAL, it means more than one. For example, *cat* pluralized is *cats.*

HOW TO GET MY LOOK,
BY ALBERT EINSTEIN

OCCUPATION _____

ADVERB _____

ADJECTIVE _____

NOUN _____

ADJECTIVE _____

ADJECTIVE _____

COLOR _____

ADJECTIVE _____

PART OF THE BODY _____

NOUN _____

ARTICLE OF CLOTHING _____

OCCUPATION _____

MAD LIBS® is fun to play with friends, but you can also play it by yourself! To begin with, DO NOT look at the story on the page below. Fill in the blanks on this page with the words called for. Then, using the words you have selected, fill in the blank spaces in the story.

Now you've created your own hilarious MAD LIBS® game!

MAD LIBS®
HOW TO GET MY LOOK, BY ALBERT EINSTEIN

Hallo. I am famous _____ Albert Einstein. Some people say I
                        OCCUPATION

look _____ insane. And zey are right, I do! But I am not actually
        ADVERB

_____. Zis is just how I like to look. If you would also like to look
ADJECTIVE

like zis, use ze makeover tips I have outlined below.

- Never comb your _____: It is supposed to look like zis! The
                        NOUN

  more _____, the better, as I always say. It also helps if your hair
         ADJECTIVE

  is a/an _____ shade of _____.
           ADJECTIVE   COLOR

- Make _____ faces as often as possible. For example, stick out
         ADJECTIVE

  your _____ in pictures. Why? Because life is fun! Do zis when
          PART OF THE BODY

  your eager _____ students photograph you. Zey will love it!
               NOUN

- Always wear a white lab _____. Zis way, you will look
                            ARTICLE OF CLOTHING

  like a real _____.
                OCCUPATION

From MAD SCIENTIST MAD LIBS® • Copyright © 2014 by Price Stern Sloan,
an imprint of Penguin Group (USA) LLC, 345 Hudson Street, New York, NY 10014.

MAD LIBS® is fun to play with friends, but you can also play it by yourself! To begin with, DO NOT look at the story on the page below. Fill in the blanks on this page with the words called for. Then, using the words you have selected, fill in the blank spaces in the story.

Now you've created your own hilarious MAD LIBS® game!

THE BIOGRAPHY OF
ALBERT EINSTEIN

A PLACE _____

NUMBER _____

OCCUPATION _____

ADJECTIVE _____

COLOR _____

ADJECTIVE _____

ADVERB _____

ADVERB _____

PLURAL NOUN _____

PLURAL NOUN _____

VERB (PAST TENSE) _____

NOUN _____

NOUN _____

NOUN _____

PART OF THE BODY _____

A PLACE _____

MAD LIBS®

THE BIOGRAPHY OF ALBERT EINSTEIN

Albert Einstein was born in (the) _____ in Germany in the year
                                    A PLACE

18-_____. He grew up to be a genius _____ with a/an
        NUMBER   OCCUPATION

_____ _____ head of hair and a/an _____ sense of
  ADJECTIVE   COLOR   ADJECTIVE

humor. Even though he was _____ smart, the people who knew him
                                ADVERB

thought he acted pretty _____. He was notorious for losing
                              ADVERB

_____ and forgetting the _____ in his equations. Einstein
  PLURAL NOUN   PLURAL NOUN

became famous for inventing things like E equals MC _____,
                                                      VERB (PAST TENSE)

the theory of _____, and the quantum _____ of light. In
                  NOUN   NOUN

1921, he won the Nobel _____ in Physics. After his death in 1955,
                            NOUN

Einstein's _____ was donated to (the) _____ Medical Center.
            PART OF THE BODY   A PLACE

MAD LIBS® is fun to play with friends, but you can also play it by yourself! To begin with, DO NOT look at the story on the page below. Fill in the blanks on this page with the words called for. Then, using the words you have selected, fill in the blank spaces in the story.

Now you've created your own hilarious MAD LIBS® game!

QUIZ: ARE YOU A
MAD SCIENTIST?

_____ ADJECTIVE

_____ ADJECTIVE

_____ EXCLAMATION

_____ ADJECTIVE

_____ ADJECTIVE

_____ VERB (PAST TENSE)

_____ TYPE OF LIQUID

_____ ANIMAL (PLURAL)

_____ COLOR

_____ ADJECTIVE

_____ NOUN

_____ NOUN

_____ ADJECTIVE

_____ ARTICLE OF CLOTHING

_____ ADJECTIVE

_____ OCCUPATION

MAD LIBS®

QUIZ: ARE YOU A MAD SCIENTIST?

Are you crazy about science? Do you go nuts for _____ experiments?
ADJECTIVE

Take this _____ quiz to find out if you're a mad scientist.
ADJECTIVE

1. Your favorite saying is: a) "Oh, _____! What did I do?",
    EXCLAMATION

    b) "It's _____!", c) "This _____ experiment went exactly
    ADJECTIVE ADJECTIVE

    as _____."
    VERB (PAST TENSE)

2. Your lab always contains: a) test tubes filled with _____,
    TYPE OF LIQUID

    b) _____ floating in jars, c) a few _____ mice in
    ANIMAL (PLURAL) COLOR

    cages.

3. Your favorite thing to do at night is: a) go to bed and have _____
    ADJECTIVE

    dreams, b) laugh maniacally while bringing to life an evil _____,
    NOUN

    c) plan tomorrow's _____-work.
    NOUN

If you answered mostly *B*s, guess what? You're a/an _____ scientist! Go
ADJECTIVE

put on your long white _____ and experiment in your
ARTICLE OF CLOTHING

_____ laboratory. If you answered mostly *A*s and *C*s, you're better off
ADJECTIVE

as a/an _____!
OCCUPATION

MAD LIBS® is fun to play with friends, but you can also play it by yourself! To begin with, DO NOT look at the story on the page below. Fill in the blanks on this page with the words called for. Then, using the words you have selected, fill in the blank spaces in the story.

Now you've created your own hilarious MAD LIBS® game!

LAB RAT ON THE LOOSE

SILLY WORD _____

ADJECTIVE _____

NUMBER _____

NOUN _____

VERB ENDING IN "ING" _____

NOUN _____

TYPE OF LIQUID _____

ADJECTIVE _____

PART OF THE BODY _____

ADJECTIVE _____

VERB ENDING IN "ING" _____

ADJECTIVE _____

ANIMAL _____

ADJECTIVE _____

MAD LIBS

LAB RAT ON THE LOOSE

Uh-oh! Last night, _____ the lab rat escaped from his cage and ran
                         SILLY WORD

amok in the science lab. He was out to get revenge on the _____
                                                              ADJECTIVE

scientists who'd held him captive for _____ weeks. First, he ran straight
                                         NUMBER

to the _____ tubes and knocked them over, _____
          NOUN   VERB ENDING IN "ING"

glass all over the _____. Then he jumped into a vat of _____
                      NOUN   TYPE OF LIQUID

and left _____ _____-prints all over the floor. Later on, the
          ADJECTIVE   PART OF THE BODY

_____ rat finally got tired of _____ around and went
   ADJECTIVE   VERB ENDING IN "ING"

to sleep under a/an _____-scope. Looks like that silly _____
                       ADJECTIVE   ANIMAL

is finally done with all his _____ hijinks. For now, at least . . .
                               ADJECTIVE

THE STORY OF
FRANKENSTEIN

PERSON IN ROOM (MALE)
_____

ADJECTIVE
_____

NOUN
_____

NOUN
_____

A PLACE
_____

PART OF THE BODY (PLURAL)
_____

NUMBER
_____

PLURAL NOUN
_____

NOUN
_____

ADJECTIVE
_____

NOUN
_____

ADJECTIVE
_____

A PLACE
_____

NOUN
_____

NOUN
_____

ADVERB
_____

VERB (PAST TENSE)
_____

MAD LIBS® is fun to play with friends, but you can also play it by yourself! To begin with, DO NOT look at the story on the page below. Fill in the blanks on this page with the words called for. Then, using the words you have selected, fill in the blank spaces in the story.

Now you've created your own hilarious MAD LIBS® game!

MAD LIBS®

THE STORY OF FRANKENSTEIN

Mary Shelley wrote a science-fiction book about a villainous mad scientist called

_____ Frankenstein. Frankenstein was a/an _____
　　　PERSON IN ROOM (MALE)　　　　　　　　　　　　　　　　　ADJECTIVE

scientist from the nineteenth _____. His greatest wish was to one day
　　　　　　　　　　　　　　　NOUN

become a real _____. So he went to (the) _____ and took a brain,
　　　　　　　NOUN　　　　　　　　　　A PLACE

some _____, and _____ legs from several dead
　　　PART OF THE BODY (PLURAL)　　　　　NUMBER

_____. Once he had sewn the body parts together, Frankenstein
　PLURAL NOUN

used electricity to make the hideous _____ come to life. Soon, in the
　　　　　　　　　　　　　　　　　NOUN

middle of a/an _____ and stormy _____, the creature awoke!
　　　　　　　ADJECTIVE　　　　　　　　　NOUN

It was Frankenstein's greatest creation, and one of the most _____
　　　　　　　　　　　　　　　　　　　　　　　　　　　　ADJECTIVE

beings to ever live—until it started terrorizing the citizens of (the) _____.
　　　　　　　　　　　　　　　　　　　　　　　　　　　　　　A PLACE

Frankenstein had to take action. He armed himself with a/an _____
　　　　　　　　　　　　　　　　　　　　　　　　　　　　NOUN

and went on a hunt for the _____ he'd created. After searching
　　　　　　　　　　　　　NOUN

_____ for months, Frankenstein finally had to give up his search
　ADVERB

because he _____.
　　　　　　VERB (PAST TENSE)

MAD LIBS® is fun to play with friends, but you can also play it by yourself! To begin with, DO NOT look at the story on the page below. Fill in the blanks on this page with the words called for. Then, using the words you have selected, fill in the blank spaces in the story.

Now you've created your own hilarious MAD LIBS® game!

ANNOUNCEMENT: THE SCIENCE FAIR WINNERS

_____ CITY

_____ ADVERB

_____ ADJECTIVE

_____ PERSON IN ROOM (FEMALE)

_____ NOUN

_____ SILLY WORD

_____ PERSON IN ROOM (MALE)

_____ ADJECTIVE

_____ VERB (PAST TENSE)

_____ PERSON IN ROOM

_____ VERB ENDING IN "ING"

_____ NUMBER

_____ COLOR

_____ ADJECTIVE

_____ NOUN

_____ ADJECTIVE

MAD LIBS®
ANNOUNCEMENT:
THE SCIENCE FAIR WINNERS

Thank you all for participating in the _____ Middle School Science
CITY

Fair. Everyone worked very _____ on their projects and it shows. We
ADVERB

will now announce the first-, second-, and _____-place winners.
ADJECTIVE

_____ won first place for her miniature erupting
PERSON IN ROOM (FEMALE)

_____, which was a model of the largest volcano in history, Mount
NOUN

_____.
SILLY WORD

_____ got second place for his super _____ miniature
PERSON IN ROOM (MALE)   ADJECTIVE

solar system, in which all the planets _____ in circles.
VERB (PAST TENSE)

_____ was given a third-place ribbon for _____ an ant
PERSON IN ROOM   VERB ENDING IN "ING"

farm using sand and _____ tiny _____ ants.
NUMBER   COLOR

That's it for the _____ annual science fair. We'll see you next
ADJECTIVE

_____ for another round of _____ science experiments.
NOUN   ADJECTIVE

From MAD SCIENTIST MAD LIBS® • Copyright © 2014 by Price Stern Sloan,
an imprint of Penguin Group (USA) LLC, 345 Hudson Street, New York, NY 10014.

MAD LIBS is fun to play with friends, but you can also play it by yourself! To begin with, DO NOT look at the story on the page below. Fill in the blanks on this page with the words called for. Then, using the words you have selected, fill in the blank spaces in the story.

Now you've created your own hilarious MAD LIBS game!

THE PERIODIC TABLE

_____
PLURAL NOUN

_____
NOUN

_____
NOUN

_____
ADJECTIVE

_____
A PLACE

_____
LAST NAME

_____
PLURAL NOUN

_____
NUMBER

_____
NOUN

_____
PLURAL NOUN

_____
NOUN

_____
LETTER OF THE ALPHABET

_____
LETTER OF THE ALPHABET

_____
PLURAL NOUN

_____
VERB

MAD LIBS®

THE PERIODIC TABLE

The periodic table of _____ hangs in classrooms and _____
                        PLURAL NOUN   NOUN

laboratories all around the _____. So what's this _____
                               NOUN   ADJECTIVE

chart all about? Well, in the eighteenth century, a chemist from (the)

_____ named Dmitry _____ created the very first
   A PLACE   LAST NAME

periodic table of _____. There are more than _____ elements
                     PLURAL NOUN   NUMBER

on the periodic table, organized by atomic _____. The elements all
                                               NOUN

have a certain number of protons, neutrons, and _____. Each
                                                    PLURAL NOUN

element on the periodic _____ has a symbol that is often the first
                           NOUN

two letters of the element's name. For example, helium's symbol is

_____ _____. Some scientists say more
LETTER OF THE ALPHABET   LETTER OF THE ALPHABET

_____ should be added to the table. Maybe someday you'll
   PLURAL NOUN

_____ one yourself!
   VERB

From MAD SCIENTIST MAD LIBS® • Copyright © 2014 by Price Stern Sloan,
an imprint of Penguin Group (USA) LLC, 345 Hudson Street, New York, NY 10014.

DR. JEKYLL AND MR. HYDE

OCCUPATION _____

CITY _____

NOUN _____

ADJECTIVE _____

PLURAL NOUN _____

VERB (PAST TENSE) _____

ADJECTIVE _____

ADVERB _____

VERB _____

PLURAL NOUN _____

ADJECTIVE _____

OCCUPATION _____

NOUN _____

NOUN _____

ADJECTIVE _____

NOUN _____

ADJECTIVE _____

TYPE OF LIQUID _____

PART OF THE BODY _____

Now you've created your own hilarious MAD LIBS® game!

MAD LIBS® is fun to play with friends, but you can also play it by yourself! To begin with, DO NOT look at the story on the page below. Fill in the blanks on this page with the words called for. Then, using the words you have selected, fill in the blank spaces in the story.

MAD LIBS®

DR. JEKYLL AND MR. HYDE

Dr. Jekyll was a friendly old _____ living in _____, England.
OCCUPATION   CITY

Mr. Hyde was an evil young _____ who did _____ things to
NOUN   ADJECTIVE

every person he met. But these two _____ were also a lot alike.
PLURAL NOUN

They even kind of _____ the same! But Hyde had a/an
VERB (PAST TENSE)

_____ power over the doctor, and became _____ evil as time
ADJECTIVE   ADVERB

went on. He was willing to _____ anyone who got in his way, and even
VERB

took _____ from the _____ townspeople. Then Hyde
PLURAL NOUN   ADJECTIVE

murdered a well-known _____! But, what a surprise—it wasn't Hyde,
OCCUPATION

after all. It was Jekyll! They were the same exact _____. Turns out,
NOUN

Jekyll had split-_____ disorder. To fix this, Jekyll did _____
NOUN   ADJECTIVE

experiments on himself so that Hyde would leave his _____ once and
NOUN

for all. But the experiments were too _____. The chemicals and
ADJECTIVE

_____ didn't work. In the end, Hyde took over Jekyll's
TYPE OF LIQUID

_____, and Jekyll was never seen again.
PART OF THE BODY

MAD LIBS® is fun to play with friends, but you can also play it by yourself! To begin with, DO NOT look at the story on the page below. Fill in the blanks on this page with the words called for. Then, using the words you have selected, fill in the blank spaces in the story.

Now you've created your own hilarious MAD LIBS® game!

LABORATORY SAFETY DOS AND DON'TS

_____ PART OF THE BODY (PLURAL)

_____ NOUN

_____ ADVERB

_____ VERB ENDING IN "ING"

_____ NOUN

_____ VERB

_____ ADJECTIVE

_____ PART OF THE BODY (PLURAL)

_____ TYPE OF FOOD

_____ ADJECTIVE

_____ TYPE OF CONTAINER

_____ ANIMAL (PLURAL)

Do wear safety goggles. They will protect your _____ . **Don't**

PART OF THE BODY (PLURAL)

light anything on fire. Always keep a/an _____ extinguisher handy in

NOUN

case you _____ set your laboratory aflame. **Do** clean the lens of the

ADVERB

microscope before _____ it. You might think you're looking at

VERB ENDING IN "ING"

a cell when really you're just looking at piece of _____ . **Don't** get too

NOUN

close to the test tubes after combining their contents. They might _____

VERB

all over you! **Do** clean up after yourself. Experiments can leave you with

_____ hands and stinky _____ . **Don't** leave any

ADJECTIVE   PART OF THE BODY (PLURAL)

experiments unattended. If you get hungry and want to grab a/an _____

TYPE OF FOOD

sandwich, stop! You need to stay put until the _____ chemicals

ADJECTIVE

in your beakers are done boiling and you've put them safely away in

a/an _____ . **Do** remember to feed your lab _____ .

TYPE OF CONTAINER   ANIMAL (PLURAL)

They're not only your test subjects, they're your friends.

MAD LIBS® is fun to play with friends, but you can also play it by yourself! To begin with, DO NOT look at the story on the page below. Fill in the blanks on this page with the words called for. Then, using the words you have selected, fill in the blank spaces in the story.

Now you've created your own hilarious MAD LIBS® game!

I NEED A NEW LAB PARTNER!

PERSON IN ROOM (MALE)_____

ADJECTIVE_____

LAST NAME_____

PERSON IN ROOM (FEMALE)_____

ADJECTIVE_____

VERB (PAST TENSE)_____

NOUN_____

ADJECTIVE_____

NOUN_____

ADJECTIVE_____

ADJECTIVE_____

PLURAL NOUN_____

ADJECTIVE_____

MAD LIBS®

I NEED A NEW LAB PARTNER!

To Whom It May Concern:

Hi. My name is _____ , and I am looking for a new,
          PERSON IN ROOM (MALE)

_____ lab partner for Mrs. _____'s biology class. My last
   ADJECTIVE   LAST NAME

lab partner, _____ , was really _____ and never
           PERSON IN ROOM (FEMALE)   ADJECTIVE

_____ our experiments on time. So I asked to switch, and the
   VERB (PAST TENSE)

teacher said if I wanted another _____ partner, I had to find one all
                                     NOUN

by myself. If you are smart, _____ in school, and always turn your
                                ADJECTIVE

_____-work in on time, you'd be a/an _____ lab partner
     NOUN   ADJECTIVE

for me. Please only contact me if you're _____ about science and
                                            ADJECTIVE

love doing scientific _____ . If this describes you, contact me at
                        PLURAL NOUN

scienceluvr1@-_____-mail.com, or just find me by my locker after
                 ADJECTIVE

lunch.

MAD LIBS is fun to play with friends, but you can also play it by yourself! To begin with, DO NOT look at the story on the page below. Fill in the blanks on this page with the words called for. Then, using the words you have selected, fill in the blank spaces in the story.

Now you've created your own hilarious MAD LIBS® game!

MY WACKY
CHEMISTRY TEACHER

_____ LAST NAME

_____ PART OF THE BODY (PLURAL)

_____ NOUN

_____ EXCLAMATION

_____ PERSON IN ROOM (FEMALE)

_____ ADVERB

_____ NOUN

_____ ADJECTIVE

_____ NOUN

_____ EXCLAMATION

_____ VERB (PAST TENSE)

_____ NOUN

_____ ADJECTIVE

MAD LIBS®

MY WACKY CHEMISTRY TEACHER

There are a lot of rumors going around about Mr. _____, our
                                                            LAST NAME

chemistry teacher. He always has a crazy look in his _____.
                                                        PART OF THE BODY (PLURAL)

Sometimes, in the middle of a/an _____ lesson, he'll shout
                                        NOUN

"_____!" for no reason at all. My friend _____
   EXCLAMATION   PERSON IN ROOM (FEMALE)

told me that he acts _____ because one time during a/an _____-
                        ADVERB   NOUN

storm he was struck by lightning in his classroom. Ouch! That would probably

explain why he is so _____ all the time and shakes whenever he writes
                        ADJECTIVE

on the _____-board. Last week, while doing an experiment in class, he
          NOUN

yelled, "_____! It's alive!" and then _____ around the
           EXCLAMATION   VERB (PAST TENSE)

room holding a/an _____ full of mysterious bubbling liquid. Maybe
                     NOUN

the rumors are true; maybe my teacher really is _____!
                                                   ADJECTIVE

AT-HOME EXPERIMENT #1: FLOATING PAPER CLIPS!

NUMBER _____

ADJECTIVE _____

ADJECTIVE _____

TYPE OF LIQUID _____

ADJECTIVE _____

ADVERB _____

NOUN _____

VERB ENDING IN "S" _____

VERB _____

PART OF THE BODY (PLURAL) _____

MAD LIBS® is fun to play with friends, but you can also play it by yourself! To begin with, DO NOT look at the story on the page below. Fill in the blanks on this page with the words called for. Then, using the words you have selected, fill in the blank spaces in the story.

Now you've created your own hilarious MAD LIBS® game!

MAD LIBS®
AT-HOME EXPERIMENT
#1: FLOATING PAPER CLIPS!

Materials:

_____ paper clips
NUMBER

A piece of _____ paper
ADJECTIVE

A see-through _____-size bowl
ADJECTIVE

A pencil

Instructions:

1. Fill the bowl with _____.
   TYPE OF LIQUID

2. Rip a/an _____ piece of tissue paper and _____ drop it
   ADJECTIVE   ADVERB

   onto the water.

3. Drop one of the _____ clips onto the tissue paper.
   NOUN

4. Use the pencil to gently nudge the tissue paper until the paper clip

   _____.
   VERB ENDING IN "S"

5. If you do this just right, the paper clip will start to _____ in front
   VERB

   of your very _____!
   PART OF THE BODY (PLURAL)

MAD LIBS® is fun to play with friends, but you can also play it by yourself! To begin with, DO NOT look at the story on the page below. Fill in the blanks on this page with the words called for. Then, using the words you have selected, fill in the blank spaces in the story.

Now you've created your own hilarious MAD LIBS® game!

FAMOUS SCIENTISTS

PLURAL NOUN _____

ADJECTIVE _____

NOUN _____

ADJECTIVE _____

VERB _____

NOUN _____

ADJECTIVE _____

SILLY WORD _____

PLURAL NOUN _____

ADJECTIVE _____

VERB (PAST TENSE) _____

ADVERB _____

ANIMAL _____

PLURAL NOUN _____

MAD LIBS®

FAMOUS SCIENTISTS

Over the years, many famous _____ have developed _____
                              PLURAL NOUN   ADJECTIVE

theories, inventions, and ideas that have contributed to the evolution of

_____-kind. Below are some of the most _____ scientists to
      NOUN   ADJECTIVE

ever _____.
          VERB

Galileo Galilei was an Italian _____ who invented telescopes and found
                                          NOUN

out a lot of information about the _____ Way Galaxy, the solar system,
                                        ADJECTIVE

and planets like Jupiter and _____.
                                  SILLY WORD

Sir Isaac Newton discovered most of what we now know about gravity. He also

wrote scientific _____ called the First Law of Motion, the Second
                      PLURAL NOUN

Law of Motion, and the _____ Law of Motion.
                            ADJECTIVE

Charles Darwin invented theories about natural selection, which proved how

different species _____ over hundreds of years on Earth. He
                        VERB (PAST TENSE)

_____ studied several species of _____ on the Galapagos
     ADVERB   ANIMAL

_____.
    PLURAL NOUN

TURN YOUR BEDROOM INTO
A SECRET LAB

_____ ADJECTIVE

_____ ADJECTIVE

_____ VERB ENDING IN "ING"

_____ NOUN

_____ VERB

_____ PLURAL NOUN

_____ NOUN

_____ ADJECTIVE

_____ TYPE OF CONTAINER (PLURAL)

_____ TYPE OF LIQUID

_____ ADVERB

_____ ADJECTIVE

_____ VERB ENDING IN "ING"

MAD LIBS®
TURN YOUR BEDROOM INTO A SECRET LAB

Follow these _____ steps to turn your boring, _____ bedroom
                   ADJECTIVE   ADJECTIVE

into a fully _____ science lab! First, put a big _____ on
            VERB ENDING IN "ING"   NOUN

your bedroom door that reads KEEP OUT! Scientists need to _____ in
                                                              VERB

silence without any annoying _____ interrupting them. Then clear off
                              PLURAL NOUN

your _____. You'll need it to hold all your oozy, _____
        NOUN   ADJECTIVE

chemicals. Gather a bunch of _____ and put them all over
                             TYPE OF CONTAINER (PLURAL)

your desk. Connect them with tubing so you can watch all the _____
                                                             TYPE OF LIQUID

run through them—_____ cool! Finally, pull your curtains shut—
                     ADVERB

you don't want anyone to see what kind of _____ concoctions
                                                  ADJECTIVE

you're _____!
       VERB ENDING IN "ING"

MAD LIBS® is fun to play with friends, but you can also play it by yourself! To begin with, DO NOT look at the story on the page below. Fill in the blanks on this page with the words called for. Then, using the words you have selected, fill in the blank spaces in the story.

Now you've created your own hilarious MAD LIBS® game!

THE MAD SCIENTIST'S SHOPPING LIST

PLURAL NOUN _____

PART OF THE BODY _____

ARTICLE OF CLOTHING _____

VERB ENDING IN "ING" _____

ANIMAL (PLURAL) _____

PLURAL NOUN _____

NOUN _____

ADJECTIVE _____

VERB _____

NOUN _____

MAD LIBS®

THE MAD SCIENTIST'S SHOPPING LIST

- Long, rubbery black _____ to wear on your hands
  PLURAL NOUN

- Giant round _____-glasses with black frames
  PART OF THE BODY

- Long white lab _____
  ARTICLE OF CLOTHING

- Two beakers—one to hold in each hand while _____
  VERB ENDING IN "ING"

maniacally

- Several cages for all your lab _____
  ANIMAL (PLURAL)

- Assorted _____ floating in formaldehyde to add to your
  PLURAL NOUN

collection

- A chalkboard and a piece of _____ to write down your
  NOUN

_____ hypotheses and equations
  ADJECTIVE

- A giant electrical power switch to turn on when you need to

_____ something to life
  VERB

- A Bunsen burner to light every _____ on fire!
  NOUN

MORE FAMOUS SCIENTISTS

ADJECTIVE _____

ADJECTIVE _____

NOUN _____

PLURAL NOUN _____

PERSON IN ROOM (MALE) _____

OCCUPATION _____

NOUN _____

VERB _____

NOUN _____

PLURAL NOUN _____

COLOR _____

NOUN _____

Now you've created your own hilarious MAD LIBS® game!

MAD LIBS® is fun to play with friends, but you can also play it by yourself! To begin with, DO NOT look at the story on the page below. Fill in the blanks on this page with the words called for. Then, using the words you have selected, fill in the blank spaces in the story.

MAD LIBS®

MORE FAMOUS SCIENTISTS

Here are a few more _____ scientists!
                        ADJECTIVE

Nikola Tesla was born in Croatia. Later, he moved to the _____ States
                                                              ADJECTIVE

of America and became an inventor. He helped create fluorescent _____-
                                                                 NOUN

bulbs so that people wouldn't have to use _____ to light their homes.
                                           PLURAL NOUN

Tesla also invented radio and worked with _____ Edison to invent
                                           PERSON IN ROOM (MALE)

things that helped electricity work.

Alexander Graham Bell was a/an _____ from the nineteenth century.
                                   OCCUPATION

His mother was deaf, as was his _____. Because of this, Bell was
                                 NOUN

interested in speech and hearing. He decided to create something that would help

people _____ each other, no matter where they were. He invented the
        VERB

tele-_____ so that people could talk to one another.
      NOUN

Stephen Hawking is a British physicist who studies galaxies and solar

_____. He has discovered a lot about _____ holes. His
 PLURAL NOUN   COLOR

most famous book is called *A Brief History of* _____.
                                                 NOUN

From MAD SCIENTIST MAD LIBS® • Copyright © 2014 by Price Stern Sloan,
an imprint of Penguin Group (USA) LLC, 345 Hudson Street, New York, NY 10014.

MAD LIBS is fun to play with friends, but you can also play it by yourself! To begin with, DO NOT look at the story on the page below. Fill in the blanks on this page with the words called for. Then, using the words you have selected, fill in the blank spaces in the story.

Now you've created your own hilarious MAD LIBS® game!

FRANKENSTEIN'S MONSTER

NUMBER _____

NOUN _____

ADJECTIVE _____

COLOR _____

NOUN _____

PLURAL NOUN _____

PART OF THE BODY _____

PART OF THE BODY _____

ADJECTIVE _____

VERB (PAST TENSE) _____

ARTICLE OF CLOTHING _____

ADJECTIVE _____

ADJECTIVE _____

NOUN _____

MAD LIBS

FRANKENSTEIN'S MONSTER

Frankenstein's monster was a hideous, _____-foot-tall _____.
                                        NUMBER   NOUN

His skin was a/an _____ shade of _____, his head was shaped
                   ADJECTIVE   COLOR

like a/an _____, and he had _____ sticking out of both
           NOUN   PLURAL NOUN

sides of his neck. Frankenstein's monster also had black lips and spiky black

hair on his _____, and his _____ was filled with
             PART OF THE BODY   PART OF THE BODY

big white teeth. His _____ arms stuck straight out whenever he
                      ADJECTIVE

_____ down the street, because the black shirt and
 VERB (PAST TENSE)

_____ he always wore were too small on his grotesque,
 ARTICLE OF CLOTHING

_____ body. What a/an _____-looking _____ he was!
 ADJECTIVE   ADJECTIVE   NOUN

MAD LIBS is fun to play with friends, but you can also play it by yourself! To begin with, DO NOT look at the story on the page below. Fill in the blanks on this page with the words called for. Then, using the words you have selected, fill in the blank spaces in the story.

Now you've created your own hilarious MAD LIBS game!

AT-HOME EXPERIMENT #2: ERUPTING VOLCANO!

NOUN_____

ADJECTIVE_____

COLOR_____

VERB ENDING IN "ING"_____

TYPE OF LIQUID_____

ADJECTIVE_____

NOUN_____

PLURAL NOUN_____

ADJECTIVE_____

NUMBER_____

VERB_____

AT-HOME EXPERIMENT #2: ERUPTING VOLCANO!

Materials:

A homemade volcano made out of plaster or _____-mâché
NOUN

A small _____ container
ADJECTIVE

_____ or yellow food coloring
COLOR

_____ soda
VERB ENDING IN "ING"

_____
TYPE OF LIQUID

Dish soap

Instructions:

1. Put the _____ container at the top of your volcano.
ADJECTIVE

2. Pour in a little bit of baking soda and some dish _____.
NOUN

3. Add a few _____ of _____ food coloring.
PLURAL NOUN   ADJECTIVE

4. Pour in _____ ounces of vinegar.
NUMBER

5. Watch your volcano _____ with lava!
VERB

MAD LIBS® is fun to play with friends, but you can also play it by yourself! To begin with, DO NOT look at the story on the page below. Fill in the blanks on this page with the words called for. Then, using the words you have selected, fill in the blank spaces in the story.

Now you've created your own hilarious MAD LIBS® game!

THE WORST SCI-FI NIGHTMARE I EVER HAD

_____ OCCUPATION

_____ PART OF THE BODY

_____ ADJECTIVE

_____ PLURAL NOUN

_____ VERB

_____ ADJECTIVE

_____ NOUN

_____ PART OF THE BODY (PLURAL)

_____ VERB

_____ COLOR

_____ TYPE OF LIQUID

_____ NOUN

_____ ADJECTIVE

MAD LIBS®
THE WORST SCI-FI NIGHTMARE I EVER HAD

I had a dream last night that a crazy _____ was trying to perform
OCCUPATION

experiments on me. He took a strand of my _____ and looked at it
PART OF THE BODY

under a microscope. Then he told me to sit in his _____ chair. But I was
ADJECTIVE

scared—there were a bunch of electrical _____ tied to it, and I was
PLURAL NOUN

afraid he was going to _____ me in it! I said, "No, thanks, you
VERB

_____ scientist—I'm getting the _____ out of here." He
ADJECTIVE   NOUN

looked me right in the _____ and said, "Don't you dare try to
PART OF THE BODY (PLURAL)

leave my dungeon! You can't _____—the door's locked!" Suddenly, he
VERB

pounced on me, and everything turned to _____. I woke up with
COLOR

_____ running down my temples. Thank _____ that
TYPE OF LIQUID   NOUN

nightmare is over. I hope I never see that _____ scientist ever again!
ADJECTIVE

MAD LIBS® is fun to play with friends, but you can also play it by yourself! To begin with, DO NOT look at the story on the page below. Fill in the blanks on this page with the words called for. Then, using the words you have selected, fill in the blank spaces in the story.

Now you've created your own hilarious MAD LIBS® game!

AT-HOME EXPERIMENT #3: TORNADO IN A BOTTLE!

NOUN _____

VERB ENDING IN "ING" _____

VERB _____

ADJECTIVE _____

ADJECTIVE _____

VERB _____

NOUN _____

ADJECTIVE _____

NOUN _____

NOUN _____

ADJECTIVE _____

VERB (PAST TENSE) _____

MAD●LIBS®
AT-HOME EXPERIMENT #3:
TORNADO IN A BOTTLE

Materials:

Water

A see-through plastic soda _____ with a cap
                              NOUN

Glitter, to see debris _____ in the bottle
                        VERB ENDING IN "ING"

Dish soap to make your tornado _____
                                    VERB

Instructions:

1. Fill the entire _____ bottle with water until it is almost all the
                      ADJECTIVE

   way _____.
         ADJECTIVE

2. _____ a few drops of dish _____ into the bottle. Add
      VERB   NOUN

   the _____ glitter.
         ADJECTIVE

3. Screw the _____ onto the top of the bottle.
                NOUN

4. Turn the bottle upside _____ and hold it near the cap.
                            ADJECTIVE

5. Spin the bottle in a/an _____-wise rotation.
                              NOUN

6. Stop spinning the bottle and admire the _____ tornado you
                                              ADJECTIVE

   _____!
      VERB (PAST TENSE)

MAD LIBS® is fun to play with friends, but you can also play it by yourself! To begin with, DO NOT look at the story on the page below. Fill in the blanks on this page with the words called for. Then, using the words you have selected, fill in the blank spaces in the story.

Now you've created your own hilarious MAD LIBS® game!

THE FIRST WEEK OF
SCIENCE CLASS

ADJECTIVE _____

LAST NAME _____

PLURAL NOUN _____

PLURAL NOUN _____

NOUN _____

NOUN _____

ANIMAL (PLURAL) _____

PERSON IN ROOM _____

ADJECTIVE _____

VERB _____

MAD LIBS®

THE FIRST WEEK OF SCIENCE CLASS

My first few days of science class were so _____ ! Our teacher, Miss

<u>ADJECTIVE</u>

_____ , taught us all about matter and energy, atoms and

<u>LAST NAME</u>

_____ , and the difference between solids, _____ , and gases.

<u>PLURAL NOUN</u>   <u>PLURAL NOUN</u>

We even got to watch a video about gravity and why things in outer _____

<u>NOUN</u>

float but things on Earth fall to the _____ ! Our teacher says that next

<u>NOUN</u>

week we're going to do our first experiment and that, if we want, some day this

year we can even dissect _____ ! My friend _____ thought

<u>ANIMAL (PLURAL)</u>   <u>PERSON IN ROOM</u>

dissecting sounded gross, but I think it sounds really _____ ! I can't wait

<u>ADJECTIVE</u>

to _____ more about science next week.

<u>VERB</u>